Resilient AS F*CK

HOW TO FIGHT FOR WHAT YOU DESERVE

DeBLAIR TATE

Resilient as F*ck
Copyright © 2022 by DeBlair Tate

All rights reserved. No part of this book may be reproduced or transmitted in any form or by any means without written permission from the author.

ISBN: 979-8-9861319-0-0

Printed in USA

DEDICATION

In loving memory of my sweet Grandma, Susie Tate,
and my Fur Baby, Scooter Caulion Tate.

TABLE OF CONTENTS

Acknowledgments 1
Introduction 3
Chapter 1: Coming From Where I'm From 5
Chapter 2: A Product of Your Environment 19
Chapter 3: The Company You Keep 31
Chapter 4: New Horizons.. 41
Chapter 5: Establishing New Mindsets............................. 53
Chapter 6: Health is a Journey 69
Chapter 7: Navigating Relationships 87
Chapter 8: Figuring Myself Out....................................... 103
The Brand: 8Figured Body 115
Conclusion: Get it, Girl! 127
The Fight. To Build Resilience 130

ACKNOWLEDGMENTS

I am so grateful for the irreplaceable assistance of the people who have helped make this book a reality.

Jasmine Womack and the EMPACT Team, The AME team, Charles Hanna, Todd Simmons, Christine Wilson, and anyone else that contributed to any part of this process. You are appreciated.

Thank you to my family, friends, and loved ones that always believed in me even when I didn't believe in myself.

Special Thanks To my Mom: I love you unconditionally.
To my Dad: I'm grateful for the connection and bond we have established.

Lola Weaver and Rhonda Hubbard thank you for being mentors and supporting me.

T. Nash: Thank you for the unwavering support. You were there at times when no one else was there. I'll always appreciate you for that.

To my team, Adrienne, IPY Agency, and Briana- Thank you both!

INTRODUCTION

If this book landed in your hands, it is not by chance. You were meant to hold the tools to your success at this very point in your life. You—yes, you.

No, I didn't ask where you came from or about the many issues you've faced along this road called life because none of that matters. What's real is that you're here right now, and you're resilient as fuck! You're awesome, incredible, the shit…any word that describes how brave, bold, and beautiful you are. If you don't feel it yet, that's okay. That's why I'm here.

By the end of this book you will have renewed confidence in your ability to conquer your fears and fulfill your dreams. All that's required of you is to pick up this book each day, read a little, write a little, cry a little, and grow a lot. I'm in the trenches with you as we navigate obstacles along the course of our evolution and the traumas we're forced to overcome—but rest assured, they will soon be a thing of the past as we focus on shifting our mindsets to walk in grace, power, and authority.

Whether you came here because of the dope ass cover, or because the idea of being resilient resonates with you, you are in for a treat. I won't hold back, and neither should you. It is time to surrender to the greatness that is in you.

No matter what it took to get here, you made it, and that is commendable. However, within this book are guidelines, pointers, inspiration, and a bold ass nudge to awaken you from a life of complacency and stagnancy to one of empowerment and success.

My journey wasn't easy, and I share my experiences throughout these pages, but what's most important is not how I started but where I expect for each of you to go because of this experience.

If you're ready, let's not delay the successful, bad-ass you any longer. Let's go!

CHAPTER ONE
Coming From Where I'm From

I grew up in the small town of Winona, Mississippi. Heard of it? It's possible for the name to have come up as some historical reference in your Civil Rights studies, but nothing more.

With a population of less than 6,000 people, there was only a single Walmart, which recently closed, and a few stop lights throughout. That's where I lived up until I anxiously graduated from high school and was liberated by going off to college. Freedom could not be sweeter than packing my bags and leaving the only place I had known as home, but the love and appreciation I have for the city and its rich history is undeniable.

Winona—small, dusty, and seemingly desolate—is known to locals as "The Crossroads of North Mississippi" because of the railroad that was built there back in the mid-1800s. It is no secret that my late grandfather had a hand in developing the railway in the region with his own aching fingers and southern heat-provoked sweat. You may not be able to tell by looking at it, but in those days, the railroad attracted settlers and businesses and Winona flourished with trade.

And there I was, plopped in the middle of this Podunk town in 1982 amid one of the greatest recessions in American history. National unemployment peaked at nearly 11%, which was the highest since The Great Depression. What does that mean for the little town of Winona? Only that what was already considered the "worst" would get worser—if that makes any sense. It's growth was stagnated because of minimal, low-skilled manufacturing opportunities offered in the region. A total shit storm when you couple it with the truth that even those with already low-wage occupations would compete with even lower-wage workers overseas. So, yep! Our unemployment rate would ultimately rise above the national average and make life for Winona's inhabitants a whole hell of a lot harder.

A Daddy-Less Past

Only with the help of my grandmother, did my mother raise me. I honestly didn't feel like I even existed to my dad. He wasn't in the picture during childhood or adolescent years, but he and my mom would communicate from time to time. When he moved up north, it seemed the distance pulled us apart. My mother would occasionally announce his plans to visit Mississippi, but I vaguely remember seeing him—perhaps it was once or twice. The inconsistency hindered us from having a fruitful relationship.

School dances and social functions where fathers were expected to participate would mean that I was escorted by an uncle or a cousin, which was often embarrassing. My father's absence—and having to rely on other male figures to stand-in for him—overshadowed even the most joyous occasions. Very early, I became self-conscious and feared people's judgment and, beyond that, I started to judge my own mother's actions and decisions that landed me in such a dreadful place. Besides, someone was to blame, right? At least that's the misdirected bullshit most immature adolescents cast onto their loving parents. I was no different. I wanted to experience the consistent love and support that others felt from their parents.

While my father's absence caused me to build resentment towards him, my mom had no room for a pity party, and didn't have the money to throw one if there was. She had no choice but to do it all on her own. Because of her hard work, I lacked nothing but answers to my father's whereabouts. Other than that, I had what I needed, and it reflected well on her. On the other hand, it was difficult to know that he had other kids and that he chose to be a part of their lives—at least from what I assumed. I would often wonder why I wasn't amongst the chosen children he'd decided to nurture. He didn't choose me. He just didn't say anything. It ruined my perception of healthy relationships and how to fulfill unmet desires.

When I was in my twenties, he began to come around–only on occasion at first. We talked on the phone and started to build a relationship, but it didn't quite heal the festering wounds of all my childhood-turned-adulthood insecurities and trauma. I was still troubled by the consistent void I felt because of his absence.

I Get It from My Mama…and Grandma Too

It would take strength and hard work to rise above inherent adversity already snowballing before I entered the world, but I had the examples of two good women along the journey. My grandmother was everything to me. I was her baby for sure. My mom was quite the disciplinarian, so whenever I got into any trouble, I ran straight to Grandma—and it was an easy trek. Luckily for me, she lived within walking distance of our place, so it didn't take long to get there at all. I can easily confirm that I was a spoiled child when it came to her because she always protected me from punishment of all sorts. She was fierce, a shield, but was always sweet on me.

There was more structure when it came to my mother, who was the type of woman that did whatever it took to make ends meet. She would often hold down more than one job at a time. Her primary occupation was in retail, and she was extremely hard-working. She exemplified her strength through her efforts, making sure that I had what I needed. I must admit that raising me required astronomical strength because I wasn't the best child growing up. As I sift through my adolescent immaturity, I see that I lacked true appreciation for her, just as many adolescents who think they have all the time in the world. I could have valued her presence and all she had done for me a lot more than I had, but it wasn't because she didn't provide for me. I rebelled against her refusal to allow me to do whatever I wanted to do and I resisted her attempts to impart wisdom into me. Her heart was for me to learn to make the right decisions in life. Of course, like any sassy, smart-mouth who thinks they've mastered life, I was defiant and didn't want to listen. My truth in those moments was that she was against me, and no one could tell me otherwise.

However, I was beyond your typical know-it-all. I felt like I was one of the kids who knew a lot more than most. So, when Mama would try to discipline me or keep me away from certain people, I saw it as control, and that was a problem for me. Don't get me wrong. I didn't have any *real* animosity towards my mom, but I was infuriated when she tried to prevent me from doing what I wanted. At that age, I saw protection as a hindrance to the life of freedom I desired.

One of the greatest issues that created tension between my mom and I was her dislike for some of my older friends. According to her, I hung out with the "wrong type" of people. Okay—I admit they were able to do things that weren't meant for someone my age, so, of course, she wanted to keep me away from them. They were able to stay out until a later hour that was way past my curfew, which was basically before streetlights would light up the pavement. Because they were older, parental control had gradually tapered off.

When I attempted to come in at nine, ten, or eleven at night, my mom wasn't going for it at all. If I wasn't at home when I was supposed to be, she would come up out of the house to find me, and that never ended well.

It's the Fight in Me

Even though I teetered on rebellion and consistently having my way, I was never one to sneak out of the house, nor did I have problems convincing my mom to let me have a boyfriend. However, I didn't date or come close to my idea of a serious relationship until I was in college. My adolescent years were primarily occupied with sporting events or hanging out with my friends. I'm far from blaming my mom for her beliefs about them. We were consistently in trouble for one thing or another, so being with them wasn't the best thing for me. Sometimes trouble would just find us, and my mom did everything she could to keep me out of the streets and away from the wrong types of people or places—especially where the gangs would hang out or where fights were prevalent. She didn't know that I was already heavily involved, and sometimes one of the ringleaders.

On occasion, hearsay regarding street fights made its way to her ears. Whenever she mentioned it, I would down-play it tremendously or would avoid the conversation altogether. If I was successful in anything at that age, it was being secretive. It's all I had to cope with the countless holes that existed for me at the time. Besides, while my mom was at work, she had very little control. The choice to stay at home from work and lose her ability to put food on the table, or to go to work to avoid the chance of me getting into trouble, was a no-brainer. She sacrificed to ensure my needs were met, but as she worked day in and day out, it came at the expense of not knowing the things that were of interest to me—good or bad.

I had an extremely low tolerance for foolishness, but I didn't consider myself a bully. That was the nature of a lot of other kids as well. We all had short fuses just waiting to be lit by some gossip or attention-seeking asshole who thought it wise to trash-talk their nemesis in front of a crowd. You could feel the tension and excitement on the way home from school when we knew there would be a fight. Only the cool kids would know where it would all go down—usually some small crevice of our neighborhood where there was little visibility and where we were hidden from people passing by that could potentially call the police or alarm our parents. And that was just elementary school life. We discovered stupid reasons to get into petty disputes, but our immaturity amplified it and made it all a big deal.

One of the biggest fights that I ever witnessed was when a girl (who is a distant relative) was the target of several kids' animosity, and they were ready and eager to fight her. She had a smart mouth and a way of entertaining guys that other girls had already laid claim to—or at least liked to some degree. One day, a group of girls double-teamed her and practically ripped all her clothes from her body before she escaped to her grandmother's house. Like the others, I was not trying to break it up. Instead, I jumped around excitedly for it to continue. For us bored, busybodies, it was free entertainment.

Rain or shine, I walked home from school every day because my mom was at work and the distance didn't warrant any other mode of transportation. The trip afforded me opportunities to be in the wrong place, and always at the wrong time. It was easy to get into foolish things, or at least be entertained by them. For instance, even if a fight wasn't on my route home, I would still follow the crowd until I saw how everything played out—a hair-pulling contest or a punch to the nose was well worth pounding the pavement in the opposite direction. Besides, I was an only-child. These crowds gave me a sense of belonging, brought me to life, and fed my secrecy—plus these kids were cool as hell. Don't judge me. It was what I knew, and I was not ashamed.

At school, I was a standout student. My education was never impacted by my involvement in extracurricular *street* activities. I maintained honor roll, and my teachers were never without praise for my performance and participation in their classrooms. I was the fight-loving, blood-thirsty chick on student council who could easily fool the best of them with my "good girl" antics. So, on paper, I was squeaky clean. School life and the street-life never conflicted.

Although I avoided my mom's consistent disdain for my friends, I knew that the company I kept mattered. I understood, to some degree, the power of other people's influence. When I was in the classroom, I was around a different group of kids than those I would frolic with outside of school. That way, I was never at risk of getting into a physical fight at school; and the beyond-school-walls fights never deterred me from doing my best in the classroom. That was just my vibe, and it was probably that way for most youngsters in town—unless they had a home with both a mother and father who were more attentive or strict.

The Sacrifice of Parenthood & Loss

My mom was a retail manager at a local store for a long time. She would move around to different locations, but for most of my school years she worked there, and it was an all-day job. As a salaried employee, she never initiated any entrepreneurial pursuits. Business ownership and self-employment weren't often heard of in our town. I can't name many people who went that route. Perhaps it is because they were taught that they couldn't afford the risks involved and that they should always have a steady job to "make ends meet." We were conditioned to make stability our main priority, and anything other than that was sheer nonsense, and laughable.

Unlike me, my mom grew up in a two-parent home, but I can't tell you if it was positive or healthy. From my youthful observation, my grandfather was a drinker, which was a consistent burden for my grandmother. He had been a rail worker for many years; and my grandmother worked at a nursing home up until she retired. I remember living with them for a short period in my very early years, and even after my mom found her own place, it was still close to Grandma's.

My grandfather passed away when I was very young. I'm not sure if he cared much for me though. I can't tell you why I would make such a weighty assumption, but it's something I heard when I got a little older. It could very well be untrue. Regardless, I enjoyed spending as much time as humanly possible with my grandmother. One of my favorite pastimes was to go to her house after school, sit on her lap and watch her favorite television shows with her—there was the *Andy Griffith Show, General Hospital, As the World Turns*, and *Guiding Light*. Time with her established what I'd come to know and understand as *family*.

My mom would pick me up late from Grandma's most of the time because of her work schedule. It was usually bath time or pushing bedtime when I would get scooped up by the exhausted, hard-working woman. When I started to participate in sports, she wasn't able to attend many of my games because of her obligation to work. No one was in the audience to cheer me on except for maybe a cousin or two who attended the same school. There wasn't a mom or dad in the bleachers for me. At the time, I didn't think it would affect me as deeply as I later realized because it was all I knew. Some of my friends had a parent, or both, chanting their names among a sea of rowdy fans. At the end of each game, I would sit with other families, or some friends, if I decided to stay for the next game. It was a temporary remedy for their absence.

While my grandmother was alive, her house was the destination for major holidays. It was tradition for all my grandmother's children from Chicago, Tennessee, and other places to celebrate each holiday in her home, especially Christmas, Thanksgiving, and the Fourth of July. We would spend the day together and have an amazing time over a spread of food and with rooms of laughter. That all changed when she passed. The unity among us quickly vanished and everyone started to do their own thing. There was no longer purpose to come home for holidays, and when some attempted, it felt very forced. Everyone started to focus more on their immediate family, and I watched the extended support dwindle away. It was just me and my mom.

Church attendance wasn't optional in my house—as in most Black homes in the Bible Belt. It was something I had to do. My family has always been people of faith, and throughout childhood I went to church every Sunday and was committed to singing in the choir. In the absence of blood connections, people in the church helped to create a village to oversee the upbringing of the children in our community. Our children's choir director was amongst them and was the real deal. She meant business. She was well known for selling her icy cups, which we called bebops (frozen Kool-Aid), back in those days. Beyond that, she was a mentor who seemed to never show us any signs of affection and we were afraid of her, but we loved that woman. We knew that if we asked her for anything, she would do it. She would cuss us out—in love. She had a way of protecting us that was like nothing we could experience at home given our resistance to our parents' reprimand.

After church service, we would often visit a particular lake about 20 miles away from our city. One Sunday, when I was 11 or 12, I experienced the traumatizing death of a good friend and classmate. He drowned in the lake, and it became my first encounter with death. We were told that he went out too far and grew tired as he waded in the deepening water. When the waves overtook him, it caused him to drown. My friends and I were very close to his family, so we attended his funeral wearing matching shirts with a picture in memory of him. It was a huge loss for our city, and it hurt for a long time. Life seemed to be a game of exits, and I experienced more people who would leave me than those who would join.

Healing the Wounds, Doing the Work

I'm jumping ahead a little here, but in my thirties, I realized that there were numerous aspects of my life that needed healing. My relationship with my father needed mending, and we finally confronted the topic of our relationship, or lack thereof. The realization occurred when I visited his sister in Grenada. We spoke of my dad, and she asked why I felt so much anger towards him. I explained that he had abandoned me and my mom, and that I often wondered why he hadn't taken care of me like he had his other children. When my aunt told me that it was a conversation that I must have with him, I had to agree. Once I talked it over with my then boyfriend, he gave me the nudge I needed to move forward and replace all my adolescent assumptions with facts by confronting the one man who had long abandoned me; and his support of this move was all the encouragement I needed to cancel the torment of all those years.

My dad's family still resided in Mississippi, so he would visit. He also had a ritual of visiting his mother's gravesite on Mother's Day. On one of those visits, we connected to discuss our traumatic past, and facing him was one of the hardest moments of my life. I had to suck it up and conquer the very thing that instilled deep insecurities within me. Most people would decide to not bother with it but, believe it or not, I wanted to have a relationship with my father. I no longer wanted to experience the depths of that void in my life, so I faced it and asked the difficult questions.

Why did you leave my mom?
Why did you not take care of me?
Did you not want me?

With patience and sincerity, he filled in the blanks and told me everything I needed to hear. To be honest, I wasn't ready for his answers. The truth was that he struggled with addiction. It hurt me more to hear his responses than it did to not know anything at all. I discovered that his absence wasn't entirely his choice. Some people can only deal the hand they've been given, and I believe that was the case for my father. Maybe it all began with decisions he made, but the consequences morphed and snowballed into circumstances beyond his control—circumstances that prevented him from being close to us and ultimately pushed him farther and farther away. I prayed and eventually dropped my resentment, which was merely the first step. I welcomed him back with open arms—as awkward as it felt initially. In this experience, I had to learn compassion, understanding, and grace. He needed it, and I knew that I would never be exempt from needing it myself.

One major impact of my father's absence was the inability to understand and nurture romantic relationships. Couple that with my mom and grandmother's inability to provide healthy examples of wifehood, I experienced a drastic learning curve to fully understand what it was that I wanted in a relationship. It took time and inner work to be confident in my worth to receive the love I desire, and to know exactly what it would require of me to maintain it. After exiting a relationship of many years, I cannot be more sure of myself, and I am grateful.

Despite the challenges, my childhood was pretty good. Everyone endures adversities that can hinder them later in life—even if they don't know it. In my case, I grew up without a father figure while my mother did her best to raise me. Unfortunately, her career meant that we would seldom operate as a family at home, and I would find a greater sense of belonging amongst the wrong crowd. The rotten cherry atop my adolescent shortcomings was the accidental death of a good friend, but any of this could cause some serious roadblocks to future success.

When it comes to the past, we can never run away. We must either confront it or let it go—which isn't the same as running away. In my case, I chose to confront some of the things that bothered me—things that created a lack of emotional support that I needed as a child—just as so many others experience. There isn't a person in the world who hasn't been let down in some way by their parents. The pain that stems from poor parenting and lack can be detrimental to the success of any of us. However, if there is still breath in your body, it isn't the end for you. Your goals and plans are always within reach, and it is time to remove the blinders and move forward.

It can be painful to look back at your life and contemplate some of the things that traumatized you, or the people who let you down when you were young. Sometimes it's hard to even remember the details of the experience. You must have the wisdom to know what you should confront, and what you should intentionally release so that you can move forward. Sometimes that wisdom is hard to find within, and it helps to have someone to guide you and help you reflect on your pain points; but don't wait for it if it's not currently within reach. Start where you are. Pray and meditate on the conditions of your past that may be a hinderance to your success in order to forgive, heal, and release them. Day-by-day, you'll become more focused, more optimistic, and more determined than ever.

CHAPTER TWO
A Product of Your Environment

Winona, Mississippi is a typical small, southern town, but I love it because it's the only place I consider home—my old stomping grounds. Our entire city was a collective *family* despite the various rivalries among us. Besides, there are disagreements and the occasional "going for blows" in most families anyway—and we were no different. In Winona, we could leave the front door open and trust that we were safe. We always knew each other's business—good or bad. Families raised each other's children, so you would get your ass whooped on sight if you were caught doing wrong or disrespecting an elder, and there was no need to wait to tell your mama what you had done. We borrowed sugar and ketchup from neighbors and would pitch in when someone was in need. We had the best mom and pop stores and home cooked meals. I grew up eating my grandmother's fried chicken and macaroni, but the corner stores cooked up the best hamburgers. That was life for me.

The closeness of being in a small city had its benefits. Babysitting services were unheard of when we could just send kids across the way to a trusted neighbor's house. There was always someone to kick it with but we were careful to not hook up with a cousin. Our community was amongst the dying village all the old folks would say it took to raise a child. And I am grateful to have been a part of Winona's.

I may have had everything I needed, but it didn't keep me from desiring more from life. Growing up in humble Winona taught me to appreciate what I already have, and then to *better* appreciate the things that I would receive. Whenever I receive a blessing or achieve success, I am more grateful because I can compare my accomplishments to previous lack and failures. I left on a quest for more but leaving Mississippi didn't change me. I will never forget where I came from.

Where the Path Leads

I would say that the tempo in Winona hasn't changed much. Some of my old friends are still there. Some left for college after high school but decided to go back home after graduation or dropping out of their program. Some got married and planted roots in Winona by starting a family with the advantage of having the support of their own parents and extended family who still reside in the city limits.

Winona never moved away from that familiar energy—there's always some drama lurking in the shadows, some arguments amongst both friends and enemies, sometimes fights in alleyways after school before track practice. Thankfully, there is not as much fatal violence as there was during my grade school years, but trouble still exists. There is not enough to do there to entertain anyone for long, and residents partake in drinking or drug use, which lures them into risky situations. It's all a recipe for foolish disaster and some residents are more than ready to pop a bowl of popcorn and pull up a seat to the shit show.

There are a lot of talented people whose gifts went down the drain because they were not given an opportunity in sports or academics, so they turned to substance abuse or simply gave up on life. It was hard to get away from Winona, but even harder to escape the mindset that was far-spread across the region. People talk about crabs in a barrel, but we must understand that the *crabs* just don't know any better. They've learned and rehearsed a mindset that's kept them imprisoned for years.

Finishing high school typically meant that graduates would stay there without any chance of future academic or professional development. Some of the people I grew up with have great jobs, but opportunities are still minimal even for the most intelligent and talented of the bunch. They simply become a product of their environment.

My first job was at a Sonic drive-in. Many of the available opportunities in Winona are service industry jobs at fast food restaurants or various retailers. There was an appliance factory there years ago but it closed. We also had a Walmart, but that eventually shut down and took a lot of jobs with it. Other decent jobs can be found on the outskirts of town or in the neighboring cities of Grenada, Greenwood, and Jackson. That didn't mean the people of Winona would relocate. They would settle into life as it is and simply *make do*. A few opened their own hair salons or catering services over the years, but they are far and few in between. I must give it to them though; they responded to the lack of opportunities in a small town in a productive and positive way. Anyone can survive the town, but once compared to what's available out there in the world, it's easy to see that Winona suffers tremendous lack.

None of us can become the best version of ourselves unless we're first content with what we already have. Dreaming big in a small town won't propel anyone to greater heights. Those who live there may have some insight into the opportunities beyond city limits but haven't exposed themselves to anything beyond the surrounding areas. Many of them leave for the military because it's an easy way out of the monotony and scarcity, and they have the (although risky) opportunity to explore more of the world.

I am Black. Check.

Okay, so—lack of employment opportunities—check. Poverty mindset—check. Drugs and drama—check. Did I mention that there is still racism in Winona? Let's just add that to the list of nonprogressive Mississippi bullshit that can ruin even the strongest person's perception of life. And I don't mean the overarching racism that plagues our nation with various employment disparities, inequality, and injustice. That's at the shallow end of Winona's deeply prejudice pool. I'm talking continued segregation through my school years in the 80s and 90s—it's just that no one called it that. Even today, racism is an unbearable force and the city is slow to catch up with the times by extinguishing it. Blacks are treated differently, and their low-level jobs prove it.

In some ways, it still has the essence of slavery. I remember an older woman who lived up the street from us. I used to call her "grandma." She didn't have her own car, so every day she would get picked up by a White woman and sit in the backseat. She wasn't permitted to ride in the front seat. When they pulled up to the house, she would go in through the back door. This behavior was normal in Winona. There were even certain shops and restaurants where we couldn't enter through the front door; and there were certain homes we would never be invited into, and certain neighborhoods we just didn't go through. We knew our place *on the other side of the tracks*.

Over the years, the schools I attended were both Black and White—but mostly Black. There was a private, Christian school, but it was only for Whites. Although it wasn't legally segregated, no one bothered to question or challenge it. That's just the way it was. It was pervasive, in-your-face racism that was intricately woven into the fabric of our existence. And do not think for a moment that the KKK would have any reason to hide in those parts; we would see cars parked downtown for their meetings, and nothing was ever said about it. We were just careful to not get caught up at the wrong place in the wrong hour.

It was obvious that Black kids were treated differently when it came to grade school punishment. If a White student got into trouble, they would get off easier if someone vouched for them. Hands down, a Black person would get punished to the fullest extent of the law for the same offence. And this pattern is but one example of inequity that seemed to trickle down to us as youngsters. It begins at the adult jailhouse. When I walked by the jail one afternoon, I noticed firsthand that approximately 99% of the inmates on the yard who were locked up there were Black. White people got into trouble too, but the jail population is just a demonstration of deep-seated unfairness in Winona.

Racism was always under the surface but it sometimes exploded in clearly recognizable events. In the summer of 1996, a retired employee of a local furniture store, Tardy Furniture, walked in and found the owner dead along with three other employees. They had all been fatally shot, and the blame fell on a former employee who happened to be Black. His supposed motive was that he had been fired a few weeks before and owed the owner a $30 advance on his paycheck. No weapon was ever found. The closest they came to having any evidence was that the bullets fired were the same caliber as the bullets that fit a gun belonging to his uncle. The jury on the case was all White. It was appealed, and the next jury had only one Black juror. The saga finally concluded in 2020 after six trials and the threat of death row when all charges were dropped. By then, he'd had the misfortune of spending more than two decades in jail.

It was later discovered that many of the witnesses who provided testimonies were not being honest. Some Blacks were desperate enough to sell their soul if someone approached them with the promise of money or to clean up their criminal record in exchange for false testimony on the stand. A lot of these people never received the money they were promised and came clean about the corruption and bribery behind this very unjust case. It was, and still is, a very hush-hush matter in the city. It was rumored that those who dared speak about anyone involved in the case would end up with their house burned down, so all was (and is) quiet.

The Glass Jar

Winona was a stopping point for those who marched to end racism and inequality. Martin Luther King, Jr. came through our town. Please note that I said, "came through." He wasn't permitted to stop. There was a church (our family church actually) that would not allow him to speak because they were afraid of retaliation by the White residents. Our residents feared the idea of progressiveness because they understood the cost of exposing bigotry and hate that kept Blacks under the submission of White authority and privilege—a cost which Dr. King would later pay himself.

Civil Rights activist, Fannie Lou Hamer, also came through Jim Crow's Winona in 1963. As she traveled with a group by bus to a conference in South Carolina, they stopped to rest in Winona. A few of them went into a local restaurant to get something to eat. Of course, they weren't served. A highway patrolman tried to intimidate them into leaving, and when they started to take down his license plate number, he and another officer started to make arrests. Hamer herself was taken to the Winona jail where she was brutally beaten and groped. When she was finally released, she needed a solid month to recover from the abuse. However, that couldn't stop her, and she went on to lead a movement—a movement that would impact the city of Winona but would not totally alleviate the deep-rooted ugliness of racism.

I was oblivious to the racism that existed. It wasn't racism, inequality, injustice—it was *life*. It was the treatment that I had always known. A butterfly that has fluttered within the confines of a glass jar all its life couldn't know that it's in a jar unless it's shown another butterfly soaring to unfathomable heights. The jar is all it knows. It's limitations is the norm.

As I became more involved in athletics, I noticed that teachers and coaches treated Black athletes differently. We had something to contribute to the school, so we got preferential treatment, which was quite bittersweet when contrasted with Black nonathletes. However, the coaches, mostly White, treated us well as far as we could tell and invited us to their homes on occasion. It was impossible to tell me they had a single racist bone in their grinning bodies. Although I cannot speak on what took place in the privacy of their own homes, there were rumors of their involvement in KKK meetings, or their abstention from condemning it at least.

Segregation was real and fully ingrained in our community's social events. Take homecoming, for example. There was tons of excitement with the boom of the band and the high energy of the football team, and we all—Black and White—shared in the experience together. However, when it came to the homecoming court, everything was Black *or* White. One Black student would be crowned Homecoming Queen, and one White student would be crowned Homecoming Queen. Perhaps it was their attempt at fairness, but it just wasn't right. The school made a huge deal about race, and it seemed that they wanted to ensure that both races felt valued and included. However, I can almost guarantee that they intentionally wanted to ensure that Blacks would be at a disadvantage and would not excel over Whites. Again, it just wasn't right. It's almost embarrassing to discuss because this was not the 1960s. This was the year 2000 to be exact—and it had been nearly four decades since the Civil Rights Act of 1964 ended segregation.

I was crowned the Black Homecoming Queen my senior year. There was another—but White. We played on the same softball team and her dad was our coach, so there was no animosity there. We all fully understood how to function in society, keep the peace, and not stir up any unnecessary mess. Besides, that societal construct didn't hurt anybody, right? (Wrong.) However, that could explain why no one ever challenged it.

Everything was separate. We had our own separate dances, senior events, and even prom. The White students had theirs at a different location and on a different day, and we were not invited. Our prom was hosted at a community hall and Black teachers were our chaperones. White teachers would only assist at the White prom. There were only rumors about the location of the White prom, so we never knew. We had a feeling where it might have been—at some fancy, big house, or maybe at the local Whites-only private school, but no one investigated. We didn't care. We weren't invited.

That tempo carried on through graduation. Church services leading to graduation were separate. We acknowledged Black students at our church, and they acknowledged Whites at theirs. We would never enjoy such monumental event together. Even our class reunions were separate and have remained separate to this very day. There is the Class of 2000—the Black People Version; and there is also the Class of 2000—the White People Version. If a student wasn't considered Black or White and were of some other ethnicity, like Indian or Asian, they would happily join the Whites.

Interracial dating wasn't typically accepted. People honored the wishes of their parents and avoided being shunned by their peers. If someone in a group of White students was dating a Black guy, those girls would avoid her like the plague and the *boy* would be lucky to make it to the family front porch let alone the picnic; but even Blacks were skeptical of letting Whites into their social circles. It was not because they weren't accepting, but because they feared the outcome and they sensed a threat to their safety. They would anticipate chaos that could result from interracial dating, and decided it wasn't worth the risk.

Friendships were different, but they still had boundaries. We played sports in mixed settings, we chatted in class and throughout the halls, but it was rare to see Blacks and Whites mingling in after school social circles unless they participated in the same sport. We would only unify if what would result could benefit the school or team. Apart from that, our interaction was kept minimal.

Shaking Self-Limiting Beliefs

Everything in Winona was Black *or* White. It's sad to reflect on those times, but it really made an impact on the woman I would become. When I later moved to the city of Atlanta, I was completely naive to a lot of things and oblivious to how mankind can move about without restriction; but it wasn't until my ten-year high school class reunion that I realized something was wrong. It's embarrassing to fathom how institutionalized racism had become in my mind, growing up in my city.

After living in Atlanta for a few years I met someone who eventually became my boyfriend. When it came time to reconnect with old classmates after a decade of moving around, I took him home to Winona for the occasion. He thought he was going to a normal class reunion. Shit—me too. When we arrived, he questioned where all the White people had gone and thought that maybe I had attended an all-Black school. I explained that the White people had hosted their reunion the previous week, and he was shocked. He asked if we could attend their class reunions, and I told him that we were never invited. A lightbulb went off and I finally realized that the continued separation was quite bizarre. For damn near my entire life, I was being treated unequally. I had accepted race-based separation as normal, and I was ignorant to how racist my surroundings were. No one had to spit in my face or call me a nigger for me to feel the pain of racism and inequality. Inferiority was ingrained in my city; it was a part of our DNA and it created a mindset that many of us would never escape.

I started to reflect on my life to discover how I may have possibly been naive about other things as well. Was I selling myself short? Was I limited in my thoughts and beliefs and expected to be treated differently because of my race? The answer is *yes*. I never expected the best treatment or fairness. I had settled in so many ways and created boundaries and limitations that didn't really exist. I was the butterfly in the invisible jar and I was finally able to see freedom beyond its façade. It was time to not only take inventory, but to cancel all the lies I had been told and reverse any hindrances in the lifestyle that resulted from my childhood conditioning.

It's one thing to read about segregation in history books and to discuss it amongst your peers as *that thing that happened* back in the day, but to recognize how long you unknowingly endured the same treatment is entirely different. It gives you a massive amount of PTSD as you move through your career and your life. You start thinking: do I always have to defend myself? Is my race a handicap? Do I have to do more, or be more, to prove my worth? The damage it could do on the human psyche is immeasurable, and I had to commit to making the repairs.

On the flip side, it made me want to do better. While most people in Mississippi see Blacks as uneducated, I was unwilling to accept that as my fate. It could only lead to a defeated existence. Due to disparities in education, Blacks are perceived as low-level-working-class individuals, which inspired me to break out of my shell. I wanted to show the world and prove to myself that where I'm from and the hardships of my past would not define me.

Here is where shit gets real. Think about your childhood and all the customs, practices, and beliefs that no one questioned, but accepted as normal. Were there certain groups who seemed more privileged? Were some of your ideas or ambitions immediately shut down because others feared what would happen if you fully pursued them? Let's sum it up with this: Is there something you would have done differently if you didn't care how others would respond to it?

It takes courage and bravery to break out of the norm—out of the condition you've accepted your entire life—but it's time to break free of the old conditioning.

CHAPTER THREE
The Company You Keep

Junior high was no different than elementary school. I was just taller. I continued to play sports, which was a core part of my identity. I was the pitcher on my softball team, one of the five starters in basketball, and I ran track. I must mention that I was also a trombone player in the school band, so I proudly represent for the band geeks of the world. Even with all these extracurriculars, I maintained good grades. The only thing that differentiated my high school experience from middle school was our ability to drive, which enabled me to get out more and visit places outside of Winona when I was bored of the local scene.

I wasn't into skipping school because I was so involved in constructive activities after the final bell; but when school let out and there were no extracurriculars to keep my attention, I engaged in activities that were not conducive to my success or well-being. Something had to fill the gaps in time and enable me to explore my rugged nature.

There were five of us in my squad of friends. We called ourselves the No Limit Soldiers, which was the name of a rap group from New Orleans. The group of rap artists talked about street life and navigating life in the NOLa. I could relate to the hustle, the drama, the conflicts, the determination to escape certain conditions, but remained proud of my *hood*. Like them, our city was saturated with drug activity, fights, shootouts, and burglaries. Rap culture had become highly influential, and we imagined that we were just as badass as the men in the music videos who flashed their gold grills and talked about the "come up." We even gave ourselves nicknames, and mine was D-Murda. Don't laugh. I was a thug, or so I thought. I behaved like one. It was cute at the time. To this day, we'll use them to get little laugh.

In addition to our core group of girls, there were cousins, big brothers, and their friends who we would hang around with on the block. This crew sometimes engaged in gang activity and real street shit that the artists rapped about. We felt closer to that lifestyle by being connected with this older crew of boys, but it would come at a cost we weren't willing to pay.

I thought it was just a typical day in 1997 when two brothers of an acquaintance—Joe and Fred—were shot and killed. I was right there when it happened—just a few yards across the street. The guys were at a corner store where we would all hang on a regular basis. The corner store had a car wash attached to it, and right across the street was a burger spot that was known for flipping some of the best patties in the city.

There had been tension building between two rival gangs in the area and being out on the streets had become dangerous. The block was hot, and people were getting hurt or would wind up dead. The brothers were in the same gang. I was at the burger spot when I heard the gunshots and feet pounding against the pavement behind the restaurant. When everything settled down, we heard screams and walked across the street to see who, if anybody, had been shot. We were so accustomed to crime that walking right onto the scene was never horrifying. One of the brothers laid in front part of the car wash. He was dead. The other was behind the car wash—and had also been shot to death. Because onlookers were sure of the perpetrator's identity, or assumed they knew who was behind the shootings, he was eventually killed in retaliation. I was 15 when I witnessed all this.

Black on Black crimes weren't the only acts of violence in our city. There were police killings, and people who were locked up unjustly as well. Desmond Harvey, my cousin, was accused of stealing carts from a White country club. The police identified him one day when he was on the corner. When he started to run, he was shot in the back and died on the scene. You won't hear any plans for protests or any march against injustice in his name, but he is amongst a long roster of men and women whose lives have been snuffed out by law enforcers. The difference—we lived in Winona. Ruffling feathers in those parts could mean repercussions that major cities haven't experienced in decades. So, like other injustices, we kept quiet about those who were given death sentences before a trial could even be imagined.

You'd think my friends and I would see the chaos and death as a wakeup call to stay at home, but we would be in the midst of it all. None of the violence could scare us away. We tried to avoid trouble, but we never knew when someone would strike. In those days, there were even dance parties that ended in fights, so City Council banned them to minimize gang activity and violence. As a result, we had to find new places to hang, but we couldn't go far. With a car and a little bit of gas money, you could get just far enough.

The Gift and Curse of Grenada

Grenada is small city less than 25 miles away from my hometown. I consider it small, but it is double the size of Winona and has nearly 3 times the population. One of Grenada's main draws was the lake I mentioned in the first chapter, but we weren't limited to the lake. There was also the strip—a high foot traffic area where Black residents would drive slow enough for onlookers to catch glimpses of their fly rides with the spinning rims or would swerve in and out of lanes to stunt; or where girls would go and get cat called and unsolicited flirtations from the boys on the block. People would park their cars along the street and play music loud enough to create a makeshift block party, and the girls and guys wore their best outfits and hairdos. It was always a party—day or night.

    We hung out on the strip in Grenada when we'd run out of things to do in Winona, or just needed a change of scenery. In doing so, we exposed ourselves to a whole different world and different people. Some friends of mine had moved to Grenada from Winona. I even had a friend who went to school in Winona who lived in Grenada, so we would make the trip to kick it with her up there. That meant we expanded our reach to be involved in more drama and more fights. The most prevalent conflict was over boys. If two girls discovered they were dating the same guy, it was a problem, and would be handled with a lot of back-and-forth trash talking that would eventually lead to physical altercation and send someone home with a black eye or few missing braids from their head. We were all territorial, and coming from another city, we were bound to set people off.

    Not everyone around me was a bad influence. I had a mentor in Grenada who was once a substitute teacher in Winona. She was a positive, guiding force in my life. She was one of those teachers who understood and could empathize with youngsters but could also guide and treat us like adults. We became so close that when I would visit Grenada, our parents trusted her to let us stay the night in her home. She let us have our freedom, but also shared her wisdom with us. She would say, "I know you're going to do this anyway, but let me teach you how to be smart about your decision," and it made me think twice about my choices. I said *think* about my choices, and not that I always made the right ones. However, I am grateful that she let me figure things out for myself without being fussy. She permitted me to explore life as a teenager without suffocating me, and I absolutely loved her.

On the other hand, I would often go to Grenada without my mom's permission. She wasn't as flexible or understanding as my mentor, so I would sneak out with older friends who had cars. Although I didn't have one of my own, sometimes I would borrow a car from my mom's friend, and he would set a curfew for me to return it. There were times when I almost broke curfew and trusted that driving fast would get me back home in time. I stepped heavy on the gas and was determined to keep my word without any regard for others on the road. I had to make it back.

I didn't understand how reckless my behavior was until my classmate's life ended tragically. I called her one day and she didn't pick up. I called her again before school and she still didn't answer. Soon after, we got wind about the car accident that had killed her. Her father was a pastor, and she had apparently snuck out of the house, stole her mother's car, and drove to Grenada. She did what we all would do to get back—go way beyond the speed limit. The car hydroplaned in the storm, and she was killed in the crash that resulted. Hanging out in Grenada too close to curfew, and the pressure to rush back before her parents awoke, caused her to travel at breakneck speed and crash. The accident was only a temporary eye opener. My heart ached for my friend, but once the initial pain was gone, so was my fear.

I enjoyed spending time with my circle of girlfriends, but I even had a crew of guys in Grenada that encouraged the mischief during my time there. Our crew was called The Clique. There was about ten of us. Whatever happened, we stood strong together. One of the guys in the squad, and my good friend, passed away from an illness. The loss was devastating because we were so young and unaccustomed to people our age passing away from illness. I saw so much death, but mostly from violence. Violence seemed easier to swallow.

I did meet a guy in Grenada during 11th grade. It was my first personal encounter with a guy but it didn't blossom into anything serious. We talked for a little while. He played sports and was popular at his school, so the ladies were quite fond of him and had me swimming in drama. While I was at his house one day, I went outside to find that some girl had come over and slashed his tires because she discovered I was there. I ended up in a fight with other girls over him later, but never fought the girl he was dating. She just talked a lot of shit. I fought her older cousin instead. Where I'm from, if you get into it with one person, you get into it with everyone connected to them. It seemed the girl's entire family slipped into the fight—her cousin, her sisters, sisters of the cousin—the whole squad. The rivalry had existed for a while, and it was time for shit to hit the fan.

We finally fought at an event the community was hosting to raise funds, or just to be social, in city hall. Multiple fights broke out that night. Chairs and tables were flying, and it was dangerous. The guys fought with other guys; the girls fought any girl associated with my guy friend's other chick. There was nothing but air and opportunity to settle any beef between rivals, so you would consider yourself being in the right place at the right time—or the wrong place at the wrong time if you were getting your ass kicked. It was an all-out battle, and the police were called. What happened next? We all ran.

During the fight, my leg was cut with a knife. I went to the hospital and received a tetanus shot in case the blade was rusty. I can't remember exactly, but there were some other injuries. However, no one went to the hospital unless it was extremely serious. It was bad, but I was alive. Fights like these only encouraged my negative behaviors, and fueled my bad-girl, street-life persona.

I started getting comfortable with drug activity when I was 17 and would continue through college. The car would be loaded with marijuana and I would ride along, and even drove at times for drop-offs. My entire life could have been changed with one wrong turn, but do you think that scared me one bit? I hope you answered *no*. I started to sell it myself once I left for college, but that career ended fast. I want you to understand that a change in scenery and new opportunities cannot save you. You must shift your mindset if you truly want to be free.

An Imprisoned Mind

Senior year was saturated with excitement to graduate and move on to a new chapter in life. Milestones like homecoming, prom, and graduation were highly anticipated, but I focused more on how I would rank at the end of the school year since academics were a big thing for me. I believe I had a balanced senior year. Being voted Homecoming Queen was never a goal, but I was popular in my school and was selected for the Homecoming Court. This type of stuff didn't matter to me. I just wanted to go as far away from home as I could possibly go.

I knew by the time I reached high school that I wanted to do something different, but I didn't know what or how. I assumed that when I graduated high school, I would go away and live a different life. I knew there was more out there, but my lack of exposure to a world beyond the one I had known in Winona made it hard to pinpoint exactly what I desired.

One thing was for sure: being a so-called "dope girl" was easy and familiar, and I stayed in the life all the way up through high school and portions of my college years. At no point did the shooting deaths of the two brothers, my friend's car crash, or the fear of getting caught, catching a federal case and possible jail time calm me down. Of course, my mom and grandma were persistent in their preaching for me to stay home and out of trouble, but there was no way to avoid the excitement of after school fights and street life unless I was dropped off and picked up. I had the freedom to run the streets despite my family's desire for me to stay out of trouble—and was eager to go off to college even if it only meant getting away from their nagging for me to make better decisions.

  I became adamant about doing something more with my life—perhaps not glamorous, but to experience life beyond what I had known in my youth. In the moment, I felt that I had no choice but to continue to run the streets because there were no other options for me—apart from my time in Memphis. I briefly escaped the streets to live with an aunt, whose son and I were close in age and we both lived there for a summer and part of a school year. There, I worked for Nike, which was a positive shift from my normal hustle, but temporary. I returned home, and back to my bullshit.

  My heart knew that I had to change to permanently get out of that environment, but it was hard to wrap my head around actually doing it and plucking up the remnants of the environment deeply rooted in me. In my first year of college, I still had the *bad girl* mentality. I was snappy, sassy, and didn't take anyone's shit. I was always on the defensive and was ready to swing if needed. I even had a restraining order put out against me the first year of college. I was a rugged girl from a small city saturated with gang violence amongst others that were so unlike me.

  Once I decided to let it all go, I finally started to change. It was still a long time coming. I ultimately joined the military and surrounded myself with people who grew up in different environments than I had. I started to transform inwardly, but I hadn't fully shaken the hood mentality, and it followed me into subsequent phases of my life. It was up to me to remove the blinders and pursue a lifestyle that was in alignment with the vision of success I had developed for myself.

Who Are You?

This question has nothing to do with your parents, your old neighborhood, any conditions surrounding your birth, or any of the fucked-up decisions you made in your past. Who you are is the consistent vision that you've been given—that place of peace, that nagging urge within you that won't let you rest and encourages you to push harder. Who are you? Or who do you wish to become? If you could have chosen the conditions of your childhood, and there were no limitations or chances of failure, who would you be?

I am here to tell you, using your past as a reason for your current lack of success is now officially an excuse. (Sorry if no one else was ballsy enough to tell you, boo.) Yes, the past happened, but you must make the conscious decision to fully pursue your destiny and your best self. Getting rid of old patterns of thinking requires intentionality and focus. Change doesn't just drop into anyone's lap. You have to want it. You have to go after it. And you start by taking inventory of those who are in your circle. Do their visions of the future align with yours? Are they motivated to do more, have more, be more? Do they support you, or discourage your upward movement? Do they encourage you to participate in risky behaviors? As the saying goes, you are who you surround yourself with. So, who are you?

CHAPTER FOUR
New Horizons

As I mentioned in an earlier chapter, there are many in Winona who view enlisting in the military as a way out. Throughout high school, I occasionally thought about joining the military. Being all I could be was in the cards, but I wasn't sure which route I would take when I started talking to recruiters who came by my high school during senior year. They often left behind a business card or two, but I would never have a one-on-one conversation. My goal was to move to Tennessee and attend Middle Tennessee University. I was intrigued by their softball team, and could see myself on the squad, but Grandma had a different vision. She was not okay with me moving to a different state alone, and preferred that I attend Mississippi State. I had two older cousins there, and she felt that family support would help me to adapt better to the environment. She got her wish when I attended for a year; but I felt like I was missing something.

Again, I contemplated going into the military after high school, and especially after Middle Tennessee was no longer an option; but my mother was against it. My only guess is that she wanted to protect me and keep me close to her. I can imagine the thoughts circling her overprotective head. However, I don't blame her. She knew that the world could be cruel. With her and my grandmother's history as Black women in the racist city of Winona, I couldn't even begin to assuage her deeply-rooted fear. Or, perhaps, it was her desire to shield me from repeating high school experiences. She agreed with my grandmother that Mississippi State would be a good choice. Besides, it was merely two hours down the road. She felt safe with that path because I wouldn't be far away if I needed anything.

I wanted to do something different. I wanted to get away from Winona, and I didn't want to come back. I knew there was more out there for me. I didn't know what it was because I lacked experience and exposure to life beyond Winona. I just knew that there was something more and I wanted to do it—whatever it was. I didn't have money to travel, so I needed to find an accessible way to expand my horizons and seek out the unknown adventures I knew were out there. I just didn't know how to get to them. My answer to that was the military—but my grandmother was adamant about me going to college. I agreed to do what she wanted for a while, and then I would do what I wanted. While I was enrolled at Mississippi State, I got in touch with a recruiter and signed up for the Air Force Reserves.

My mom was not as protective as my grandmother. She was far from happy that I had signed up behind their backs, but she did not try to stop me. She was supportive. After all, joining the Air Force wasn't a bad decision. They simply had to accept the fact that I was growing up and they would have to let me go. I had an uncle and cousin already in the military, and it gave the women in my life some comfort. My cousin was almost killed by stepping on a landmine overseas, but the incident happened after I joined. Otherwise, they probably would've gone all out to prevent me from joining. He was in the Army but told me that it was no place for a woman. He explained that the Air Force would take care better care of me. My ASVAB test scores were sufficient to get into the Air Force, so the decision to go made sense.

Only after I already had my date to head out for basic training did my grandmother discover my new path. My recruiter was on board to come with me to tell her. And believe me, she wasn't thrilled with the news, but she knew I was an adult. She asked the recruiter to make sure he took good care of me. Believe it or not, he did. Some recruiters will say what they need to say to get recruits in the door, but I can honestly say my recruiter made sure that he honored his word to my grandmother, even after she passed away. He made sure my questions were answered and that I was not given the short end of the stick.

I was able to complete my first semester of college, and then I left for a semester and summer of basic military training at Lackland Air Force Base in San Antonio, Texas. When recruits get off the bus on day one of BMT, they don't know what to expect. Superiors start to yell right away. On that night, I thought to myself, *Oh my gosh... What did I get myself into*? I'm sure lots of Airmen feel this way, but then it all becomes routine, and you start to make friends. My mindset was not so positive initially, but it eventually started to change.

You can do this! You can finish this!

I would give myself frequent pep talks. I knew there was so much love and support from family back home, which helped me get through it as well. However, we were not allowed to stay in touch with family. We couldn't even call home until week five, which was the week before graduation. And graduation just *might* present an opportunity to see them.

Reflecting on where I'd come from and knowing that I wanted to do more in life, was enough to give me the mental fortitude to push through basic training. I realized that if I didn't get through it, there was a chance that I could be back home in Winona, Mississippi wondering where else my life would go. In a sense, it was *do or die* because I knew I had a bigger purpose. And this was my one shot to get there. I was trying to break barriers, and I knew it would take sacrifice. I certainly didn't want to go backwards.

I mentioned how racism and segregation was a part of my childhood and adolescent experience, but everyone was treated like shit at BMT. Race didn't matter. You were talked to like trash, but that was the whole point. They would break you down to build you back up. I was the dorm chief, so I was the go-to liaison between the training instructor and the other Airmen. My training instructor was a Black woman who was very mean to us, but I believe it was by design.

On My Grown Woman Shit…Or Not

BMT was certainly transformational. I grew up getting into fights, so you could say drama was a part of my aura. However, when I returned home after BMT, my friends thought I was a totally different person. I would say, "Yes, ma'am," and "No, ma'am." I thought differently about life and my goals than I had before my experience in training. I can't say that I was 100% changed, but I was more disciplined, had better time management, kept a tight schedule, and had organized my priorities. I had become more polished by the structured environments of BMT and tech school unlike the undisciplined freedom I'd had back home. The new environment forced me to create a routine that would greatly benefit me and my new, rigid lifestyle. The hour I would go to bed, or wake up, and the things I tolerated in conversation were all different. I was growing into a mature woman.

The fact that I had played several sports certainly made BMT easier, but it was still a challenge. I struggled, but for those with no athletic background, it was harder. I was able to push through. Some were sent home because they couldn't complete the physical component of training. Sometimes it was the mental part that hindered them—like discipline or lacking the ability to tell yourself that you can get through it. That's where the coaching I received in sports, and the experience of participating in structured organizations like band, helped me through this leg of my journey.

I returned to college to pick up where I left off, but I was behind the eight ball. If I desired to graduate on time with my class, I would have to double up on my courses and take 18 to 21 credit hours at a time, go to summer school, and make up for the semester and summer I had spent at BMT. I worked hard and was very motivated. I even held jobs at a local hotel as a front desk representative and at a college bookstore on top of a heavy academic load, playing softball, and balancing life as a college student.

It was stressful as I tried to keep it all together, but at the same time, I was still involved in some of the same types of hijinks I had been doing in high school. I hung out with a couple of girls, including my roommate. Sometimes our drama would, of course, involve guys. So, when I came back from BMT, a guy I met freshman year that played football had a new girlfriend. I thought we would pick up where we left off, but that's when the high school drama resurfaced and my lack of maturity was made evident. I guess I hadn't moved far from simply being young and dumb. I was still getting into altercations and fights just as I had in high school.

I later showed interest in a sorority –Delta Sigma Theta— and that became a big part of my life. The sorority put me around girls that were more even-keeled when it came to temperament. Some of the girls that I pledged with were just like me—you know, if something happened, it would go down. Together, the military and the sorority environment really helped me grow up. I wanted to be a classy girl. I didn't want to resort to violence but the fight was still in me, and I was often tempted. But those structured environments helped me to become a better person.

I often reflect on how college was one of the best times of my life between the amazing friendships I created and the parties. I was never really into drinking but dabbled lightly with marijuana. Once I got into the military, drug testing motivated me to eliminate it once and for all. I was academically sound, so that didn't give me any grief. To top it off, being in a sorority meant that you were popular on the yard.

Inspired to Create Change

Despite all the perks of college, the segregation I had experienced in Winona followed me to a new campus, and I had become more aware of it. For one thing, the sororities and fraternities were separated into White and Black groups. The Whites had their own frat houses and sorority houses, the Blacks had theirs. It's weird that it's right in front of us and people don't talk about it, but instead treat it like it's normal. Like back home, there was a cafe near campus that still had a Whites-only water fountain, and a door that only White patrons could walk through. They started to integrate a little more by allowing anyone to walk through that front door, but if you were Black and you walked through it, all eyes were on you. It was obviously weird as fuck, so few would do it. Clearly the service Black customers received was different. Some servers wouldn't even wait on a patron if they weren't White. The world at large wasn't like this anymore, but our small southern towns were majorly behind the times. It's just built into the culture. It's a known fact that Mississippi was the last state to ratify the 13th amendment to end slavery—almost 150 years after the Civil War. Sure, nobody had slaves anymore, but we still had segregated social events and Whites-only doorways.

These experiences motivated me years later to become an Equal Opportunity Representative (EO) in the military. I wanted to ensure there was zero tolerance for discrimination against anyone based on race, gender, nationality, or whatever. I maintained that position for eight years and was driven by my ability to understand what it is like to be on the receiving end of discrimination. I wanted to make sure the people around me never had to experience any maltreatment. I didn't go into that position because I wanted to exclusively fight for Black rights. My drive was for everyone to be treated fairly no matter who they are—for everybody to start out on the same playing field, and so that nobody feels more entitled because of skin color or gender.

There were a lot of strikes against me in the military. I had come from a small town in Mississippi, I'm Black, and I'm a woman. When anyone aspires to climb up the ranks, they quickly learn that it's a White man's world. And if you're not educated and on your A-game, you won't make it. Whether you admit it or not, race is a big factor. The scary part is how hidden it is. Many times, choices are made because of biases, but they're dressed up for other reasons. Someone will say, "Oh, we chose this person because of *these* reasons." And if there is ever a complaint or a suspicion of bias involved, I would ask for them to help me understand their decision-making process. Sometimes they would have their ducks in a row and could justify a discriminatory decision, but sometimes they couldn't and would be called out.

There were many formal complaints, and to this day discrimination is a part of the military culture. I dealt with a lot of cases—even outside of Mississippi—where people were still hanging nooses. There was one case at another Air Force base where a commander thought it would be funny to hang a noose in someone's locker, which shook up the entire base. For somebody to think that behavior is funny demonstrates how little they understand the symbolism and pain behind the prank. However, these moments can become learning opportunities.

I'm no fan of pulling the race card to complain about something, but sometimes it's just obvious that race was a part of a decision. Personally, I'm more vocal about confronting discrimination when I see it. I don't allow myself to be mistreated. Even if someone looks at me differently because of who I am, I don't allow it to go farther. I challenge things that need to be challenged, and I speak up. This could be a gift and a curse for many reasons.

I didn't start as an EO in the Air Force. No one can pick their career path as a newly minted Airman. We could create a wish list of what we wanted to do, but we couldn't pick our paths unless we entered as a professional—like a doctor or mechanic. For someone like me, I had to get in where I fit in. Once you're in the military and you've gotten your foot in the door, you can cross-train yourself into different roles if the availability is there. The truth is, I didn't really know what I wanted to do anyway—just as I didn't know which major to pick in college. I was just escaping the life I'd once had and was winging it. I was coasting and trying to figure it out as I went. I didn't have a plan for what I wanted to do, but my scores, my location, and availability sent me to Keesler Air Force Base in Biloxi, Mississippi.

Moving On…and Going Through

At each transition, I was never afraid to branch out on my own, but my family felt it would be better for me to be under someone's wing. I went to Biloxi and everything worked out fine for a long time. It was a new chapter of life to come from college and straight into a full-time job, but I frequently went back to campus for football games and social events.

The weather in Biloxi is tricky. It's right on the Gulf of Mexico, and when the hurricane season comes, it really comes. I had gone back and forth to Biloxi for years as a part of my training, but I had never lived there full-time. At that point, I was living in an apartment right on the beach, and it was something else to see the storms plowing through or hearing hard rain. We witnessed the power and aggression of nature. Wait… Did I mention that my first role was in the 41st Aerial Port Squadron where were tasked with loading pallets to be sent overseas, as well as pallets that hurricane hunters would use to drop things into storms? If not, there you have it. Hurricane hunters are real, especially in those parts. Don't worry; my job was far from risky. I was a personnel, so I primarily ran the administrative side of the house.

The final straw for me was Hurricane Ivan, which was the storm that wreaked havoc right before Katrina. (Thank goodness I was able to leave before that.) During Hurricane Ivan, we were all evacuated to my college city and were forced to stay away from Biloxi for a week. When I returned, the apartment building I lived in was completely torn up. Luckily, my personal belongings inside were fine, but the structure of the building was compromised by the weather. So, that was the moment I said, *I don't think I can do this*.

The courage I once had to do my own thing was no longer there. I knew I had to live someplace where the weather was not so uncompromising. I had developed some friends in the area and they understood. On the other hand, I was there alone. I had no family and facing all those hurricanes alone was unnerving. The weather was too unpredictable and sometimes very extreme. I was ready to leave Mississippi but didn't know where to go.

I reached out to a college roommate who had moved to Atlanta. Atlanta had never been on my radar, but when I called her and we got to talking, I suddenly knew that I would move there. I asked if I could live with her until I found some place to stay and she agreed. That was all I needed. Well…that and a job. I looked online and took the first thing available to me.

At the end of my tour, I became part-time in the military and moved to Atlanta to start my new life. I slept on my friend's couch in her one-bedroom apartment and continued to do so until I earned enough money to have my own place. I put most of my belongings in storage. I had no plan, no idea where I'd be living, and very little money saved; but nothing would stop me from getting away from those places that no longer served the woman I was destined to become. Don't get me wrong—I still just didn't know exactly what I was looking for. I just knew I was chasing a better life. My horizons had started to open up.

Knowing When It's Time to Move

From knowing when to exit a relationships to taking the right action and request a promotion, it is imperative that we identify shifts in our experiences that are nudging us to move. We were created to evolve and not to stay in the same place our entire life. It doesn't matter what gives us the push; if you can acknowledge that something is telling you to move, then do it.

We are solely accountable for the outcome of our lives. If you desire to move on for greener pastures, safer environments, or just a better life for you and your family, make no apologies for it, and never give a damn about what other people may think. Make sure you are doing what's best for you. Your goals are your goals.

You were born into this world alone, and you won't take naysayers or any of their opinions with you. Live for you!

It is time you take inventory of times in the past when you made decisions based on what other people wanted you to do, or moments that you made decisions out of fear. Take control of your life and pursue only what you desire.

CHAPTER FIVE
Establishing New Mindsets

It's challenging to see men and women, hands out, asking for change on the side of the road. The impact of the homeless population is not the only reason for my burden—it's also knowing that many of them are men and women who served overseas in the armed forces just as I had. The difference is that I sought help for each condition that plagued me as a result of war, in the mind and abroad. Some of them went to war, and never fully returned from it.

Even if you've never stepped foot in a war zone, there are attitudes and behaviors that you can implement to help you win on the home front of your mind. The three that I cling to most are self-discipline, focus, and gratitude. Each of them have enabled me to blossom and evolve into the woman I am today.

Self-discipline is the key to success. You could wish and pray, and even put in the hard work, but if you lack discipline—which is to work consistently to achieve a specific goal—it will be an incredible challenge to get what you want. Be consistent! Discipline means that no matter what it takes for you to have success, whether you must cut back on spending to save money, eliminate poor food choices for a healthy body, or minimize time with friends to focus more on building or business, you do it!

So, let's take some inventory. In what ways do you lack discipline? Think of character traits or habits you may possess that demonstrates poor discipline on your part. Are you pressing the "snooze" button so frequently that you're consistently late for work?

Do you reach a new Monday week after week, and make a new promise to start that diet on the next Monday? Do you have plans to write a book, but haven't sat still enough to get it done? These are all indications that discipline may not be your strong point. Stop that shit.

Let's be honest here. We all have room for improvement, and we start by acknowledging what those areas are. Once we recognize areas of weakness, it is imperative that we create small goals to improve it. Don't be fooled. There is nothing wrong with starting small. If you want to diet and shed weight for 90 days, start with a single week, and then build from there. If you want to write a book, start with completing a paragraph each day, and then a page, until you've written each of your chapters. If you plan to spend more time with your children, start by intentionally going into their rooms or calling them into the living room to hang out with you for a half hour. Spending time with loved ones doesn't have to be an expense or cause you to travel from where you already are. Break down your goals into smaller pieces so that they're less intimidating and appear easier to manage.

The Pitfalls of Pain

Some people mistake resilience for strength. Don't get it twisted; strength is an admirable quality to have, but you're not required to always be strong. It's okay to be vulnerable. It's okay to acknowledge that you're going through something and that you don't have it all figured out. We all have issues. Life happens. However, you don't have to dwell in that place. It's ridiculous for people to insist that we must be strong, take anything that comes our way, and act as if it doesn't affect us. The hell with that notion. Darts are being flown towards us daily, and it's not your ability to bear them that speaks volumes about your character, but your ability to get back up when you've been struck down. That's what it means to be resilient—to be human. It's how you move when things happen that makes you resilient.

Understand that life is going to happen. For as long as you're living, many things will come to test you. Some will cause pain and deep hurt that you must be able to accept. You must acknowledge it, acknowledge your feelings about it, pivot and move forward. Never allow a situation to take you to a low point where it's extremely difficult to come back from it. Bounce back! There's no time limit, but it shouldn't get to a point where pain and disappointment drags on and starts to affect your life.

Acknowledgment is major when it comes to being resilient because some people believe that sweeping things under the rug is the answer. At some point, the shit eventually hits the fan and you will recognize all the buried bones in your closet that you refused to deal with. Acknowledge and accept!

I fine-tuned my ability to be resilient when my grandmother passed away. Prior to that, nothing really knocked me down. That situation knock me down, took me out, and everything else. It happened. I was greatly impacted and couldn't function for a long time after that. I knew I had to figure out a way to keep pushing. I wanted to move on because I knew I needed to. People lose their parents or others who are close to them, but I lost the person who was most important to me. It took me a long time to get to the point where I felt like I was okay.

My grandmother passed of heart failure in 2003 when I was in my early 20s. It just wasn't her time—way too soon, and very unexpected. I wasn't ready. She went into the hospital for some minor ailments and never came out again. I felt empty. She was like a best friend, and we talked all the time. Knowing that she was no longer there rocked me to my core. She was the person that I felt cared most for me, and who understood me the most. And then she was gone.

So, I bet you're wondering how I dug myself out of the hole of painful loss. I wish I could say it was simple, but I will say that knowing how to avoid sinking is well worth the effort. Here is how to cope with loss without losing your shit:

1. If coping with death has been difficult for you, it is imperative that you start to look at things differently. Search your memory bank for all the positive moments you shared with them. Understand that no one was created to live on this earth forever, and we were all born to someday pass away. We must learn to release them. What hinders a timely release is regret. Perhaps it's not even the pain of their loss that you're grappling with, but your inability to say goodbye or wishing that you had given them more time may be a burden.

2. I am a firm believer that everything happens for a reason, and God consistently orders our steps. If you've lost a career position, know that even when it doesn't look positive many blessings come in disguise and that this is exactly where you need to be. I think back to the events of 9/11—how some people didn't report to work or was detoured by one thing or another, and ultimately avoided catastrophe. Some "failures" and "no's" are divine protection. God removes things out of your life to make room for new things, and sometimes we don't see the big picture. As humans, we want instant gratification. So, when things are not going exactly the way you want, just be patient. Trust, believe and pray. This may just be your opportunity to birth something new.

3. When a romantic relationship comes to an end, you must take accountability for your part in the failure. If he/she left you high and dry, remember that *you* chose to be with them. Forgive them for their part but, most importantly, forgive yourself for the part you played as well. And let it go. Accept the fact that people have the right to choose whether or not they want to stay in a situation. Know that when people walk out of your life, it's not always a bad thing. They were only meant to be there for a set amount of time, or for a particular reason. God is doing something, and we must be still and wait and see.

We must learn to practice detachment by knowing that things are going to happen, people will come and go, and there are no guarantees. When you understand what it means to detach, you can love deeply and cherish each moment you spend with someone, or in a particular position, without clinging to it as your lifeline. Your thoughts will align with, "I know that this job provides income for my household right now, allows me to flourish in certain ways, and I'm able to use my skills, but if I am no longer here, I can be somewhere even better." Sometimes we hold on to things for dear life that God is trying to get us to release. Everything is always working out for your good. Believe it.

Have Focus & Self-Control for a Change

Most people can't control their thoughts, which creates their actions, and they ultimately land in a place of stress and anxiety. It is important to practice mindfulness if you're not already. It means to focus your energy (or attention) on the here and now. What can be done in this moment that would create bliss, fulfillment, or peace? Sometimes it's nothing at all but stillness or holding someone's hand. These are moments when you quiet your thoughts and listen for that quiet, inner voice that gives you clarity and direction, or when you listen for nothing at all. The problem with most of us is that we feel like we must always have something going on. We're afraid of silence, so we fill it with being overactive or will gossiping nonsense. Don't fall into this trap.

In addition, there tends to be many distractions that come to make us lose focus. I hear of a lot of things that people wanted to do, but they haven't done it for whatever reason. They're distracted. It could be in the form of a man that comes up to you like a shiny penny. It could be friends. It could be technology and social media. Anything that causes you to lose sight of what you desire to do is a distraction.

I could live in Mississippi and have a deep desire to get out. *I have to go! I have to do something better than what I'm doing right now, and I have a plan in mind!* However, if I don't keep my eyes on my goal, I could end up falling off or going a different way. Someone or something can cause me to lose focus. It takes being intentional and disciplined to stay the course. When you recognize that you're off course, jump back on! It's not going to be an easy path. It's not going to be a straight road because things will consistently try to throw you off your focus. Once you realize that you're no longer on the right track and your mind is wandering, recognize and acknowledge it, and then get back on track.

You can't be everything for everybody. And neither can I. As the Vice President and founder of my motorcycle club, I'm very active. To write a book amid my daily demands and leadership duties, is tough. It takes real focus and determination to get to the end of a project that is beyond the realm of your daily grind, but it's possible if you minimize or totally remove the distractions.

Technology is a major distraction for me. So, I purposely no longer use my phone when I wake up in the morning because it throws off my entire day. People will call me wanting to have conversations and discuss some negative topics—you know who they are in your life. Because I know people can cause distractions, I pick and choose when I want to talk to people. If I need to stay focused, unless I sense it is a dire emergency, I don't answer. I may call back later, but I must set clear boundaries and allow things to happen on my terms when I'm focused and determined to reach a goal or stay on track.

My previous relationship was a struggle because we didn't see eye to eye on where my priorities lie. I was doing everything that I believed I needed to do for the relationship, but it wasn't in line with my goals. Know that if you and your partner are not on the same page, negativity can easily seep in and the distraction factor is greatly amplified.

There are situations beyond your control, especially issues that your family may come against. For instance, if a family member loses their job, it may create a distraction because you're now coming up with ways to help them instead of focusing on your own goals. There is nothing wrong with helping, of course, but be mindful of how extending yourself impacts your plans. Parenting can also be a distraction from what you truly desire. There are no days off when it comes to being a parent, so you must balance it with building the dream. Fear is also a distraction from what you hope to achieve in life. And finally, one of the greatest distractions is comparison. A lot of people compare themselves to the progress of others and how they're succeeding. They become more focused on everyone else's "dream life" instead of building their own. Keep your eyes on your own prize.

A focused life is…
1. Organized and structured.
2. Low stress because you're more in control and less scattered.
3. Perfectly set boundaries that limits people's access to you to minimize distractions.
4. Understanding the power of the word "no" and using it.
5. Staying the course.
6. Proactive—refusing to procrastinate so things never pile up.
7. Not seeking validation and being confident in who you are and what you have to offer.

If you couple consistency with focus, you are sure to be a force to be reckoned with. Some people assume that things are just going to happen at the blink of an eye, or that opportunities will just fall from the sky. If they don't consistently work towards their goals, they won't get very far. It is very important to stay the course and not give up when things get tough. Refuse to get frustrated and overwhelmed at the sign of failure and know that everything is always working out for you.

If consistency is a challenge for you, you must address your belief system. Do you believe you can have what you desire? Do you believe you can succeed? If you can see it and you can believe it, then you will naturally align to it and remain consistent in your actions regardless of what comes at you. You will swat down any objection to your vision with a confident, "I believe I can achieve this, so I will keep going."

Consistency causes you to sacrifice or step outside your comfort zone. There are days that you may not want to do anything to work in the direction of your goals, but consistency stretches you to keep moving. It is common to have a career or work odd jobs as you build your own business. The objective is to never abandon your personal goals, even if you must sacrifice a night out with friends or an extra hour of sleep at the end of your night. Put it this way: if you don't clock in at work tomorrow, they will simply hire someone else to do the job. Who can you hire to take your own place? (I'll wait—NOT!) No one can accomplish this goal but you!

Attitude of Gratitude

Gratitude gets you far, but I think that's where a lot of people lose sight. Many of us see the glass half empty instead of half-full. Most of us don't understand the power of gratitude. I practice gratitude every single day and I started doing it about four years ago. I found myself complaining about things that I didn't have and failed to acknowledge the things that I did have.

I once hosted a birthday party, and I remember complaining about who did not attend, and didn't realize that I was discrediting the people who did come. It made them feel a certain type of way, as if they were not enough. From that point on, I understood that I needed to cherish the time I spend with others and be grateful for those who show up for me versus dwelling on disappointment when they don't.

If you focus on the positive and identify the things that you do have, it is easier to be grateful. When you can acknowledge that there is money in the bank as opposed to saying, "It's just not enough in there," you'll see your life transform as you invite in more miracles.

Life continues to happen and we all have issues. You see, there are people in wheelchairs with no legs and we constantly complain about trivial things while we take health and vitality for granted. We're lazy—don't want to get up and move while some people wish they had legs. So, when I think about things that I have that others wish they had, my whole mindset changes and I am instantly grateful. When you show appreciation for the things that you have, it allows room for other things to come in. It allows the doors to open for fresh opportunities because you appreciate those you already have. If you don't appreciate what you have, you're not going to gain anything more.

Every morning, I wake up and say, "Thank you." Gratitude starts my day on the right foot and helps me to be a better person—one that others want to be around. I'm not filled with negative talk, so my positivity radiates outward and draws others to me. It also helps me to build better relationships with others because I communicate my thankfulness to have them in my life. People want to feel appreciated, so not taking them for granted goes a long way. In addition, gratitude has improved my mental and emotional health and has minimized my stress. Overall, I have a better quality of life.

My life shifted. I'm more intentional with people, and I never embrace negativity or he-said-she-said talk. I don't even entertain it. When someone speaks negatively about a person, I always have them look at it from a different perspective. And they hate when I respond by asking if they've actually talked to the person they're discussing. It helps them to understand my boundaries, and they typically won't return to gossip. People no longer call me with the drama, and I'm not involved in any nonsense because they know how I move now. I am respected on a totally different level, and they come to me to seek advice. They come to me when they're down and out. They come to me to uplift them.

Here are some ways to incorporate more gratitude into your day:

1. Express gratitude upon waking. I start my day with prayer (and there's a difference when I start my day with prayer than responding to messages and emails on my phone).
2. Refuse to complain.
3. Know that gratitude is contagious. Saying "thank you" or offering a smile can make someone's day and will cost you nothing.
4. Do this gratitude exercise by answering a single question: If I could only continue to have what I am grateful for today, what would I be grateful for? In other words, imagine the things that you didn't say "thank you" for today being gone tomorrow. Would you then be grateful? For loved ones? For health? For your home? For your vehicle?
5. Celebrate the small victories. A lot of people have huge visions and goals and may lack appreciation for reaching smaller milestones. So, instead of saying, "I want to be a multi-millionaire and a mogul in the industry but I'm not there yet," it is better to say, Wow! I just registered my LLC! Let me pop a bottle of champagne!" Every little step that you take in the direction of what you desire should be celebrated, that's gratitude.
6. Be positive! Positive energy spreads and allows doors to open.

Fixed Mindsets Vs. Growth Mindsets

When my coaching group is in session, I discuss the difference between a fixed mindset and a growth mindset. A growth mindset is reflected in someone who is optimistic and easily perceives what is necessary for life and success. People with a fixed mindset are prone to failure because they always feel like there's a limit to what they can do. They don't see themselves as great and dismiss their talents or down themselves. They think they're not good enough, and typically don't like to be challenged. When they're frustrated, they may give up.

A person with a growth mindset welcomes challenges. They like to try new things and easily step outside of their comfort zone. They are open to constructive feedback to become better and are seldom defensive—unlike fixed mindset folks. They're not afraid to take risks and, even if they fail, they don't look at failure as failure. They take it as a lesson.

Which do you possess?

It is important to have the right people around you. You can't have the same people around who reflected your fixed mindset behaviors and climb to greater heights in life. Start paying attention to those in your circle. I surround myself with people that are successful and have something to offer, and I can also identify what I can offer them as well. What do your closest friends bring to the table?

Mentors are a blessing, and so are relationships that result from networking. Be intentional about what you're looking for and don't latch on to those who cannot contribute to where you are now or the person you are becoming. Have people that you look up to for their example a growth mindset, or feel free to continue to cling to those with fixed mindsets and see how that goes for you.

When you are valued by others, they tend to hold you accountable for your progress in a way that may be hard to do on your own. With the right people around to tell you when you're falling off, or to guide you when things get tough, it's easier to weather life's storms. Everyone needs at least one person who challenges them to dream big and to pursue wholeheartedly. Not everyone can be that for you.

You Wanna Be Like Who?

Authenticity. Damn. Where do I begin? Being true to your own values and yourself, regardless of the pressures to be like others, is tough in this social media age. As you maneuver through life, there will be many influences. There will be many situations where you may feel like you need to be something that you're not. You may find yourself amongst a group of people and feel like you can't be yourself. It's discomforting to feel that you must have a certain status or a certain look to be accepted.

The best feeling in the world is to no longer feel like you must change who you are to be acceptable. Being you and being honest regardless of who's around is priceless. Be the person that everyone can come to for honesty and transparency. Personally, my friends and family know that I'm going to be real with them. I won't tell you what you want to hear. This journey has been too expensive to be fake.

Sadly, we take our examples of perfection from social media, and it's saturated with inauthentic people. Social media life and real life are two different things. Sometimes you can be so engulfed in life and the people around you that you end up compromising yourself and your values. For instance, if you don't normally smoke or drink, but the crowd you find yourself around makes it easier for you to slip into slush mode, you have stepped into people-pleasing and inauthenticity. Know who you are, and never apologize for it. There is nothing wrong with connecting with people who have different values than you if you don't allow their presence to make you lose yourself.

Authenticity helps in the pursuit of the dream because it requires that you first know yourself. There are many who don't fully know who they are, or what it looks like to be real, because they consistently conform to what society sets as the standard. Your goals are your goals, and you cannot live your life for anyone else. When you're authentic, you don't waver from what you want and are more focused. People who embrace their uniqueness don't allow anyone else to dim their light or tell them they're not good enough. Don't allow others to push their goals or their values on you.

Refuse to care about what other people think. Stay true to yourself. Once you get to the place you desire, you can look back and be proud that you didn't compromise who you are. You didn't compromise your integrity. You didn't allow your character to be assassinated. You don't have any regrets or embarrassing moments because you were true to yourself. People will respect that.

No DNA is identical. We're all created differently. We all grew up with different experiences, observations, perspectives and so forth; and we should use that to create what no one else can. No one outside of you can achieve and do exactly what you're going to do, so never get lost in trying to mimic other people, or you risk the opportunity to fulfill the one thing you were designed to do.

How to *Get a Life*

The things that you are motivated to do should give you life, and not take life away. That said, be sure that your intentions throughout your pursuit of success are genuine and comes from a healthy place. All your aspirations, dreams and goals are already in total alignment with what you have done your entire life. There are skills, habits, and values that you've picked up that grants you insight into your purpose and what will lead to the most fulfilling life. It's time to reflect on what makes you tick, what brings you the most peace, what makes you confident and self-aware.

At times, we worry. We have no clue how our greatest passions will come about. Maybe you're saying you're not qualified enough, smart, or attractive enough, or have enough money to pursue it. I am telling you to leave the details in the wind and wholeheartedly pursue. We cannot know how everything is going to unfold until we're looking back at it. Fearlessly follow the breadcrumbs to your own success.

CHAPTER SIX
Health is a Journey

After I moved to Atlanta, I started working at a gym and participating in fitness competitions (but that's for another book...stay tuned). During the time, I made a persistent effort to truly find myself and figure out my life's purpose. *What the hell was I put on this earth to do?* We tend to wander when we don't understand our purpose or create real intentions to fulfill them. Even in college, I had very little direction. I moved how and when I wanted to move, but there was nothing that made me say: *This is what I want to do for the rest of my life.* I was winging it and letting things just fall into place as I went. In Atlanta, I had worked full time as a loan officer, part time as a sales rep at the gym, at the smoothie bar, and then I became a professional fitness competitor, but I knew there was even more that I could do.

Becoming a massage therapist was an idea I explored for a few months before I acted on it. I knew that massage therapy would tie into my career as a personal trainer. And it became obvious that my mind was focusing on personal branding and building a whole package of what I could offer others. I finally understood what it meant to have a sense of direction, and I had the faith to push me out of my comfort zone.

After I enrolled in massage therapy school, I started to discover health issues. Up until that point I would have sworn that I was the healthiest person to walk the face of the earth. I realized my ailment in the most random way. While I was gathering vegetables in the frozen foods section at Kroger, I noticed that when I encountered something cold, my fingers would go numb. It was weird. They would have no feeling and then turn blue. If I held a bag of frozen vegetables, my skin would turn dark purple, and so would the tips of my fingers have a purple hue. Initially, I brushed it off. *Doesn't everybody's skin change colors when they get cold?* I thought. These episodes went on for some time. It probably had been happening for a while, but I started to notice it more often.

One day, I was finally able to put a name to it and start to understand what it was. A part of the massage therapy curriculum is an immersive in-depth study about human anatomy. Everything doctors should know about skeletal structure, massage students must know as well. You start to feel like a doctor yourself learning every muscle and certain skin diseases—just in case it was relevant to a future client's condition.

During class, we had to stick our hands into a bucket of cold water as a part of the lesson. Looking at those buckets, I knew my fingers would become numb. Before we stuck our hands in, we had a lesson on various autoimmune diseases. What would it look like for a client to have rheumatoid arthritis? What would it look like for them to have Raynaud's syndrome? We casually talked about it in class, but everything the teacher described about Raynaud's checked off a list in my mind. I came to know that diseases and ailments have no age bounds and didn't just impact old people.

After we discussed the symptoms, a lightbulb went off. I said, "I think I have this!" The teacher looked at me as if I was crazy because I blurted it out in the middle of the lesson, but I was convinced. I showed them. I stuck my hand in the water and my skin started to turn colors that it shouldn't. The blood vessels in in my fingers started to open up, which constricts the flow of oxygen and made my fingers numb due to improper circulation. I was starting to develop ulcers at the tip of my fingers because of it. If the condition worsens, sufferers can lose the tissue at the end of their fingertips, and they can shorten. By the way, it's very painful. There is an intense burning sensation that requires sufferers grab hold of something warm or run hot water over their hands to get the blood vessels to return to normal and get oxygen through.

    I started to read up on Raynaud's Syndrome a little bit, and what I saw worried me. It's more than just getting cold hands. In some cases, it's a symptom of something bigger. In fact, for 80% of the people who exhibit symptoms of Raynaud's, an underlying condition like lupus, or rheumatoid arthritis, or other autoimmune issues could be to blame. Before I went to the doctor, I Googled about it. Of course, Google can scare the shit out of you because it always lays out worst case scenarios. Without knowing any better, or any knowledge of what was going on with me, I feared the worst.

    For the first time in my life I was afraid, and I did not know what would happen to me. I was even more concerned because autoimmune disorders run in my family, and I had two aunts—my mom's sisters—pass away from lupus. Her younger sister where I got the middle name, Fayette, passed in her twenties, as well as her older sister. The older one, who was my favorite aunt, withered away before our eyes. She and I had similar personalities. She was sick for a long time, and never told anyone what was going on with her, so she suffered in silence. She hid it until she couldn't anymore. The last time we were together, we buried a cousin in Chicago that had been gunned down as a result of gang violence. Like I said before, this type of life ran deep in my family and the results didn't always end well. He had been involved in gang activity and was shot and killed in the streets.

    I rode up there in the car with my aunt. She didn't look like herself. We knew her to be a beautiful woman, but the steroids she took to counter her condition changed her appearance. She decided to stop taking the medication, but didn't tell anyone, and no one knew how sick she really was. This type of response to failing health can be detrimental to any family. Although it's understandable, keeping information like this from loved ones can leave them with a void and unanswered questions. I believe it's best to make peace, which she didn't.

What was strange is that she started to give away shit like it was Christmas. She got rid of jewelry, clothes, and furniture. She visited her children and spent extended amounts of time with them. We know that's a red flag—when people start to do things that's out of their norm. Weeks later, she passed. It was later obvious that she was checking off boxes on her list, but we didn't realize what was going on. She had never told us that she had lupus. She just moved forward with life; it was the doctors who told us.

Knowing that my mom's two sisters had lupus, I was very concerned. My primary care doctor referred me to a rheumatologist and I had to go through several tests and bloodwork. I told the doctor that I may have Raynaud's, and he was like, *You think you're just going to diagnose yourself?* But I was positive I had it.

My boyfriend at the time was very supportive and helped me get through all the tests, but I didn't tell anyone else what was going on. I went through a few doctors until I found a good fit. The first doctor put me on a lot of medication, but I didn't fully know what was going on because the tests results had not come back.

When the test results came back, I thanked God they only indicated that I had Raynaud's. The lupus test was negative, but they did not know if Raynaud's was the primary condition or a symptom of something else. They couldn't tell me if lupus would surface eventually or if something else could later develop. They only said they would monitor my situation. My exact diagnosis was non differentiated mixed connective tissue disease. Doctors placed me on several medications, and I am tasked with getting tests and bloodwork every few months for the rest of my life. Today, I'm on watch and care. This could have easily broken me, caused me not to value life, or to give up. I didn't. I held my head up, and I kept going, and advise anyone who is facing a hardship to do the very same.

When I went for doctor's visits, I was scared but I didn't tell my mom. I was her only child, and her two sisters passed from autoimmune disease. Instead, I adopted my favorite aunt's stance and didn't want anyone to know. I had developed a strong demeanor and a hardened exterior. I didn't want anyone to treat me differently. I didn't want anyone's pity.

Trying to Catch a Health Break

Unfortunately, I started to develop other conditions as well, including very bad episodes of vertigo. When I first experienced it, I had started working with IBM as the lead project manager for an IT group who did refreshes on computer systems. We were working on a Hilton property one night when I started to feel dizzy. The room felt as if it was spinning ten thousand miles per hour. I was vomiting and had to go to the restroom repeatedly, but I was still trying to do my job and push through, but eventually I had to just go to my room.

I was in the bathroom with severe vomiting and diarrhea, and I couldn't hold myself up. It was the worst feeling I had ever experienced, and I wouldn't wish it on my worst enemy. I called my boyfriend to pick me up, and I had to be wheeled out of the hotel in a luggage cart because I couldn't stand. They put me in the car and took me to the clinic. The doctors thought the episode of vertigo was connected to Raynaud's, so they admitted me into the hospital and injected me with Meclizine and an IV. They started to run bloodwork to see if anything latent inside of me was becoming active, but they couldn't find anything specific. I had to visit more doctors and have meetings with a Rheumatologist. I started to think that my health was declining, since I experienced one thing after another.

The initial episodes of intense vertigo went on for about a week, and I still have vertigo episodes today. They're still an issue at times. I never know when they'll come but I can feel them coming. I've been to all types of doctors about it—neurologists, several ENTs (Ear, Nose, Throat doctors)—and have subjected myself to all sorts of brain scans, tests, and anything else you can think of to figure out the cause. At first, the doctors thought it might be the medication. Later, they thought I might have Meniere's disease. They wondered if it was related to an autoimmune issue. They tried everything under the sun to figure it out. I desired to make sense of it all as well. I was still a personal trainer and worked for IBM. On the outside, I appeared to be a hard, strong, resilient person that people could look up to, but on the inside I struggled with my health. Only my boyfriend at the time knew about my condition, so I mostly carried the weight of my situation myself. Even still, I never let him know completely how I was feeling each day.

I still see the doctor every few months to have tests run and for them to monitor my health. There are still no real answers on what causes the vertigo, although I've narrowed it down to what I think is stress. I believe that stress can trigger my vertigo, whether it's negative stress or positive stress. For example, one time I was the event planner for a huge 5k and got vertigo a day after the event. Thankfully, over the past seven years my lupus panel has been negative. I've had some decline in essential vitamins, but that could be the result of me not eating meat for some time.

What my rheumatologist concluded is that my health was impacted by positive lifestyle changes I'd made in support of my nutrition and fitness. She thinks that when I started to pay attention to what I ate and worked out regularly, I helped to slow down whatever condition could become active in my body. My healthy habits around diet and exercise helped create a barrier. I had omitted all sugary drinks, gluten, and fried foods, and was living a healthy, clean life. Because of the way I trained, it was very likely that any potentially negative attacks on my health were mitigated; and the issues that I had already developed could have been worse if I had been more careless with my body. My Rheumatologist said that whatever I'm doing, I should continue to do it; but of course, she can't promise that nothing will surface.

One question I was consistently asked by doctors was whether I drank alcohol. I did not and, just like my healthy eating and exercise habits, may have contributed to keeping any dormant conditions at bay. The reason I did not drink was actually because of my uncle who passed away from alcoholism. He had lived with my grandmother for most of his adult life, and I remember him drinking all the time. He would come home disrespectful and belligerent and would stress my grandmother out to the point where she felt there was no hope. There were times when she would put him out if he got too drunk and began to bother people, but she feared the chance that he would get into a fight in the streets and not be able to defend himself in his drunken stupor. People on the streets are not as compassionate as family. Ultimately, she decided not to put him out and tried to make up her mind about what to do. The internal battle took its toll on her health as well.

The entire situation turned me off to drinking. My grandmother was everything to me. To see how alcohol would cause him to treat her made me never want to drink alcohol. My uncle was a quiet guy. He didn't talk much. However, when he got drunk he would turn into another person—yelling, cussing. The next morning he would wake up like nothing had happened, and as if he hadn't acted a damn fool the night before.

It got worse, and it is my opinion that he contributed to her death because of the stress he caused her. The stress of her having to deal with him amongst other things shortened her life. After she passed, he became sick. His vital organs didn't function properly. His ability to breathe deteriorated and he had to use oxygen. He slowed down on the drinking but it was too late, and he passed away at a relatively young age of 43 because of alcoholism.

Sucked it Up and Kept Pushing

I have nights when I get cold and it hurts. People say, *Look—your hands are purple!* It's very painful, but I hide it because I don't care for their comments or pity. It's hard to say if hiding my health struggles is me not being genuine, or if it's simply my prerogative to hide it; but here I am—ready to tell others about mental health, the importance of taking care of themselves, and how to be accountable. I was able to do that without being vulnerable or real. Perhaps I was not ready and there would be a time and place to share my health challenges. It's always a battle to figure out how to share a story, and how much to share. In my case, I didn't want others to feel sorry or question me about it. In my mind, I was invincible and untouchable, but God will humble you quickly.

I was almost kicked out of the military because of my health. At that point, we had tried numerous medications until we could figure out what worked. Some of them gave me headaches; some of them made me sleepy; and some of them made me unable to function during the day because I was so tired. It took months and months of misery on my end to get to a point where I could get a grip on it. The doctor had to take up dosages, take down dosages, change medicines altogether. The doctor's experimentation with my medication landed me in a tricky situation.

Before prescribing medications, she would ask if I suffered joint pain, which was a symptom of autoimmune disease. I replied *yes*, but we were not on the same wavelength. I considered the fact that I work out frequently, so of course I have joint pain. I regularly pushed myself to the limit. However, she correlated that pain with potential arthritis, and then asked me to take a very serious drug.

Methotrexate is typically given to cancer patients, but is also a disqualifying drug in the military—even with a prescription. The disqualification is automatic, but I was not aware. I hadn't even gotten it filled when I asked my doctor-friend about it. He was surprised that she would prescribe a drug for cancer patients. I had requested to go 100% off meds, but the doctor feared that if something became active in my body she would not have time to stop it with a new prescription. She figured it was better to leave well enough alone and continue the medication.

Every year, we would do comprehensive medical exams for the military, and I had to make sure they knew what was going on with me, including anything my doctors outside of the military had prescribed. When they reviewed the paperwork, they discovered the prescription for Methotrexate. At the time, I was going through the Officer Training Program and needed to meet criteria for them to approve my medical and physical health. When they saw the prescription, they told me that I could not complete the program and become an officer.

Cold fingers should not stop me from being an officer, I thought to myself. That wasn't it. The Methotrexate was a red flag, and they were not going to push my medical records through or offer their approval for me to become an officer. And worse, my head was on the chopping block to avoid a medical discharge from the military entirely, because they would assume I was sick with cancer.

Becoming an officer was off the table, and I was losing my cool. I went to my commander and anyone else who would listen to try to figure out what was going on. My rheumatologist wrote a letter, but it was still a year-long battle to prove to them that I didn't really need to take Methotrexate. Doing so was difficult because it was in my medical records. Therefore, the military would have to put me through their own tests and evaluations to determine whether I was as sick as they assumed based on the medication she'd prescribed.

Thankfully my wing commander and command chief fought hard for me. I explained what happened, and they talked to my doctor. I had to prove that my joint pain was from working out, and they needed a second opinion to verify it. They watched me closely—like I had a scarlet letter on my chest. It barely went in my favor. I was not able to go through with OTC and I was coded, which means that I am essentially non-deployable. If I ever deploy overseas, I will have to be close to a medical facility. To this day I'm fighting to get the code removed. On the bright side, I was able to stay in the military.

A Life Full of Silver Linings

You know what they say, *when one door closes another one opens.* All the circumstances that resulted in the OTC rejection opened the door to becoming a first sergeant. My command chief said to take the rejection as a sign that it was not the direction I should go. Eventually, my first sergeant role led me to becoming a first sergeant instructor, which is a title I hold at the time of writing this book. I was a first sergeant for over three years in the squadron and was still having bloodwork and tests every 3 to 6 months and continued to be attentive to anything out of the ordinary.

I ultimately went overseas as a first sergeant. My command chief put my package in to get deployed, medical approved it, and somehow missed the code. Afterwards, they gave me a waiver. It was the higher ups that said I could not deploy, and not my base. I deployed to the Middle East after all and broke barriers they said I couldn't break.

There were still some struggles over there with my physical and mental health. I experienced a lot of vertigo episodes while deployed, but I did not alarm anyone to what was wrong with me. Some nights, I suffered through horrible bouts of room-spinning vertigo. It was also winter, and the Middle East is freezing cold in January and February. You might not expect it in the desert, but the wind blows at cut-your-throat cold temperatures. And I was out in it—moving from point A to point B with troops. I had consistent aching, burning hands, yet I was determined to prove myself. I wanted to show them that I could do it—that I could be over there without medical attention.

I was there for over eight months. As soon as I came back, I put in paperwork to remove the code because everything they said I couldn't do I had already done it. Unfortunately, the doctor that handled my case and pushed for the code to be removed had retired. Therefore, it is an ongoing process.

I'm still monitored by doctors, but it's steady. I still have vertigo episodes, but not as often—maybe once or twice per year. It's basically become a lifestyle for me. It's a routine of bloodwork, medications, and checkups. Every day I pray that nothing changes. Every time I go in for bloodwork, my heart pounds and I pray, because all it takes is one time to get results you don't want. I never know what each month will hold, but thank I God that it's so far, so good.

The Fight is Not Just Physical

As a first sergeant at the medical squadron in the Middle East, we went back and forth to the flight line. The flight line is the aircraft runway. We were the hub for injuries and casualties to pass through. Our medical team handled dignified transfers, which meant that they helped to bring home the bodies of fallen soldiers. Being involved in that, and the trauma that came along with what I experienced over there, created a whole new health issue for me—with my mental health.

I had to be strong, to not only deal with my personal health ailments, but to manage the issues other people had as well. I didn't let anyone know about the nights I miserably laid in bed as the room spinned 90 miles per hour and caused me to throw up, just to get up and go to work the next day like nothing happened. I had a very important position because I was first sergeant. The command chief, the commander, and I were known as the triad. We were the top three people who ran the squadron, so I dealt with all the people and their issues to help meet their needs.

I was the go-to person for the medical squad, and I saw a lot—too much actually. I observed the injuries of those who had stepped on landmines and gotten an arm torn off. I saw 18 and 19-year-old kids going home in a body bags, and a few with a pregnant wife at home. I talked to troops with severe depression who wanted to committed suicide and had even tried. Luckily, no one was successful in their attempt, but we found one young woman incapacitated in her room after taking some pills. Her husband had reached out to someone who then contacted us and told us that she threatened to commit suicide. When we found her, we had to pump her stomach.

It was my job. It was what I had to do; but it started to affect me. I was numb to it at the time because I was one of the few in charge, and I knew the job had to be done. Someone had to be there when the team had to do the dignified transfer and get the soldiers back home. Injured men and women and dead bodies came from all over the Middle East—Afghanistan, Kuwait, or anywhere overseas where we were fighting Osama bin Laden and Al Qaeda or ISIS. Anywhere there was boots on the ground, there were injuries and casualties coming back.

There were a lot of moving pieces to the War on Terrorism. Some injured patients headed to Germany for treatment and used our location as a hub for medical transport. It was even my duty to go to troops at 2 or 3 in the morning and let them know that a family member back home passed away and would facilitate getting them home to attend the services. I dealt with other people's depression, divorce—you name it. When there was a problem, I was the point person to deal with it. There was some support from my supervisors but handling most issues and moving troops to the right place was my job. The squadron had to run properly, but how much it affected me wasn't clear until I returned. All that I experienced in the Middle East had taken a toll on me and was amplified by my own personal health issues.

When a soldier returns from deployment, the military keeps its eyes on them. They fully understand how a lot of people come back affected by what they see over there and, in some cases, they develop PTSD. Initially, I thought everything was fine, but those around me noticed some red flags in terms of my behavior. I had become very irritable. If you were talking to me and I didn't have time for what you were saying, I'd cut you off in a minute. I was moving through my day like a freight train and never really stopped to reflect on anything. I was probably afraid of what I would think about if my mind became calm.

I was resistant to the idea of therapy and was offended that anyone would think something might be off with me. When I finally decided to try therapy, I just wanted to see if there was anything to what others were saying; and it turned out that my deployment and my experiences affected me deeper than I was willing to admit at first. I had to work through the issues it created within me. And for those of you reading this book that have been deployed, or who have gone through a traumatic situation, you know it never fully goes away. To this day, I have a hard time sitting in certain places, or with my back to a door. I also no longer feel comfortable with male doctors. These changes have become my norm—my way to cope—even though it may not be healthy at all.

Don't Forget the Mental

Health is more than skin deep. You must consider your mental health along with the physical. Without it, you're not fully healthy. Understand that being a healthy individual has no end; it's a journey and a process. Consistently evaluate where you are.

How am I feeling today?
Does the experience I had then continue to pain me now?
Have I gotten progressively better or worse?

Your inner peace matters. There are many uncertainties in life, and sometimes you must live through doubt, do your part to live well, and have faith. However, there are professionals who can help guide you to the answers you seek.

Although Black Americans are not often introduced to the concept of psychology and mental health therapy, these are tools we all need. Magic can happen when you get out of your own head and discuss your worries, fears, anxieties, thought patterns, and behaviors with a licensed professional who can help you gain clarity, understanding and peace.

Consider this: If you've used your hands to do the work and have been consistent in your pursuits, but have yet to see success, consider there is some mental blockage that must be addressed.

What are your beliefs?
What are your deep-seated fears?
What created them?

It's okay to need help. No one is exempt from traumatic experiences that result in a need to heal and release them for a brighter, more successful tomorrow.

People—especially Black people—assume that a need for therapy marks us as broken, vile, or weak. We assume that something must be wrong with a person who has regular calendar visits with a therapist. When I returned from overseas, I felt the same way. I experienced a lot and I didn't realize how it had affected me until it was too late. I started to act differently. I wasn't myself and others started to notice my defensive behaviors. Many who suffer from PTSD don't even realize what's happening, and I was one of them.

I needed someone to help me through the process, and therapy was that help. Don't get me wrong, licensed, clinically-trained therapists are amazing, but don't discount pastors, ministers and others who work as counselors when you're in need of help. How do you know when you're in need of assistance?

1. *Having signs of depression.* When your emotional state negatively impacts your day-to-day functions, you may benefit from talking to someone about it.

2. *When you identify miscommunication issues within your relationship.* With a counselor, you can work together to learn better techniques to communicate.
3. *When other people's opinions and expectations begin to weigh you down* and you desire to regain control.
4. *When it's hard to navigate from where you are to where you want to be.* If you experience stagnancy, it might be a good time to discover what may be holding you back by talking to someone who can get to the root of your issue.

Black people are taught to be tough because life is generally hard for us. A relationship issue, depression, or mourning the loss of a loved one isn't sufficient to lose sight of the work there is to be done. We're told to suck it up, and not told to go to therapy. Counseling never becomes a priority because the expense outweighs the importance in the Black community. When you're trying to make ends meet, paying someone to tell you about your problems is not a good investment of your resources. And since we are also under-represented in the field of psychology, it further drives a wedge between already non-trusting people and their desire to seek help from those who look nothing like them and who may not understand.

There is no health without mental health. As a Health and Wellness Coach for over seventeen years to date, I wish I knew then what I know now. I would have gone a different direction when it came to my clients. I was trying to fix them when it was impossible for me to fix them. The problem wasn't about fitness training or eating healthy. The problem was whatever was going on inside of them. I tried to get them to love and accept themselves, and it seemed almost impossible for them to see themselves as I saw them.

They wanted to heal emotional wounds with physical changes, and it just doesn't work.

I am always curious to ask people: Why did you alter your body with surgery? No matter what they say, I can recognize how new societal norms impact mental health and drive men and women to the operating table. Perhaps a lack in confidence could point at childhood trauma, sexual abuse, or neglect, and it's not because your body is unlovable. This is an area where professional help can be of benefit.

Yes, I get it. We wear "Strong Black Woman" as a badge of honor, but please fully understand what strength is before you label yourself and struggle because of your misconception. Strength is recognizing that something is happening and still being able to have a positive outlook. It is also knowing when to say, "no" and when to take a knee and take care of yourself. Strength is knowing when to ask for help. What strength is not—pretending to never experience pain, or that feeling hurt is unimportant. If it affects you, it is important. You are important. When you know how important you are, it is easier to set boundaries, take self-care days, start new adventures, relinquish fear, and put aside any possibility of intimidation. You can stand alone and feel as if there is an entire army behind you.

CHAPTER SEVEN
Navigating Relationships

When I relocated to Atlanta, I understood that I had to tread lightly and be careful. It was a culture shock to go from a small city where I knew everybody and no one really tickled my fancy to one saturated with sexy, successful men. There was no need to jump in headfirst, however. I couldn't look at the first shiny penny that came my way and think that was it, right? I thought I would take my time, be patient, date, get to know people. I asked the right questions to understand them before committing to someone, but was that enough? Did I fully know what I needed in my relationships, or what I would be required to pour back into it?

My most recent relationship was honestly my first real relationship, believe it or not. I dated before—one or two guys in college—and had a couple of situations here and there, but it was never anything that serious or solid. We eventually lived together, and our lives became intertwined. We were damn near married, but I don't believe I ever learned how to date. I hadn't learned what a healthy relationship should look like or what I was supposed to look for in a good relationship. I was just winging it, and I'd be the first to admit and take ownership for several mistakes I made along the way.

The mature and experienced me also acknowledges that I put up with way more than I should have. Sometimes I knew things didn't feel right or look right, but I was down for my man and was committed, so I thought that I was supposed to just keep going. The whole learning curve of that relationship molded me into the person I am today to know exactly what I want, what I don't want, and what to even look for in others. I was able to form my own list of red and green flags. Don't misunderstand; they are not a one size fits all on the preference level. They stem from seeing enough of what you don't like and knowing what you do like, which helps you choose a partner you think would be good for you.

One of my gifts and curses is the ease of forgiving. I'm a very forgiving person regardless of what someone may have done or said. Those I adore could easily play on my emotions and make me feel responsible for a clash in our relationship—like I contributed to it and we're both learning. I would find ways to take responsibility for someone else's bullshit. What I failed to understand is that there are others who don't know what healthy relationships look like either. With neither of you knowing how to form appropriate expectations, you can assume that the most toxic relationship is what romantic love is supposed to feel like.

In our ignorance, we hear traditional marriage vows and strive towards them. "For better for worse" doesn't apply in all conditions, and especially if you're constantly forgiving and forgiving. It should be clear that there are no real boundaries that say, "Hey, I'm not going to tolerate this!" Instead, you just go through it, and you feel how you feel at the moment. You may have a conversation about it with your partner, and then it's as if it didn't happen and it's swept under the rug. When it's a new day, you're back to acting normal. And it's just that—*acting* normal.

When you don't discuss issues that you have, they continue to fester. Over time, it creates resentment because there was no genuine forgiveness but some noncommunicative forgiveness. It's easier to be in a comfortable place versus being in an uncomfortable place where you're not talking or experiencing some other dramatic friction.

Not So Flawless

One of my flaws that resulted from how I grew up was not fully understanding how the things I would do affected the other person. I didn't know that my actions could make them respond or feel a certain type of way. I discovered personal characteristics that made me reflect on what it means to have a partner, and I learned that when you are in a relationship, you can't just be about you. In the same sense, it's not supposed to feel forced. When two people are in a situation and know each other's love language and make a valid attempt to support them in that regard is a beautiful thing. However, it's unhealthy if nobody's walking away because they've grown comfortable and would rather be with them and unhappy. Some who think they're happy really aren't. They gather many years under their belt and look back to realize that they probably should have walked away a long time ago. It's okay to walk away from relationships—and it took me a long time to learn that.

Leaving doesn't make anyone a bad person. Sometimes it just doesn't work out. No one can make things fit that's not supposed to fit. It's okay to have your preferences. Realistically, if you're looking for that perfect person on all four squares, I don't believe he exists. You must find somebody that you're willing to grow with and know what you're not willing to tolerate. Sometimes when people have motive, or they do things over and over and keep apologizing for it, it's not worth it. Repeating the same behavior is a problem. If I consistently do something that I'm not told is an issue or a deal-breaker, once it's communicated, I'll apologize and then do better. Therefore, it's okay to walk away because perhaps that person is just not the person for you if you're stumbling over numerous red flags and deal breakers.

Those Damn Deal-Breakers

Fuck the norms and know what you want! It seems that in our society, marriage validates the female existence, but not the male existence. Do not allow society to dictate how you live your life. Divorce is okay if it leads you to a place of peace, but most people refuse to leave terrible relationships because they're afraid their actions will be frowned upon. Some people decide to get married simply because it's the "American way" to have a spouse, two kids and house; or simply because they felt pressured by parents or loved ones to settle down.

When you make the decision to enter a relationship on any other grounds than the fact that you just want to, what will keep you there when times get hard? Or when there is work to do? When you're going through a rough season? You can't just give up every time things get bad, but it should present an opportunity to learn more about each other and to grow. It is always your right to decide whether you want to stay and work through any obstacles, but knowing why you started can serve as a reminder and equip you with patience for the healing journey within your relationship. On the contrary, if you ever decide to exit a relationship, know that it doesn't have to end with fussing and fighting. You can love them from a distance, remain friends, and even give them guidance without being in a relationship with them.

Here is a list of reasons I personally believe it's time to exit a situation:

1. *If you are being abused.* No further explanation is needed; but if for some reason this isn't self-explanatory, tell someone about it and exit as quickly as you can. There is no entanglement great enough to suffer physical pain to maintain it. Seek help, and leave.

2. *When the bad starts to outweigh the good.* When it's to the point where the relationship is not fun anymore, and is constant work, it might be time to pack your shit and cut your losses.
3. *If you're constantly in battle with each other and all the butterflies are gone,* you may want to reevaluate how you truly feel about each other, and just let go. Sometimes you can get back into a groove, but other times you can't.
4. *When you no longer look forward to seeing each other,* and you're just comfortable because you've been together for so long. Understand that when you're in a relationship, being away from that person is foreplay as well. You should foreplay all throughout the day in conversation, or via text messages. If something reminds you of that person, tell them. Send them a song or something. It builds anticipation to see each other again, even if it's not for days. If you barely talk, or the conversation is dry, and you have nothing to talk about or to look forward to, that's a problem. I get it—starting over is bitch, but don't allow the time you've already invested compel you to waste even more of your precious time.
5. *You no longer look for ways to make that person smile* because you're always mad, or simply don't give a damn.
6. *You get annoyed by the smallest things that the other person does.* Your lover can't even sleep without you complaining about how inconsiderate he is for taking too much of the covers. It's bad when every little thing that person does is a problem for you. Leave, boo.
7. *When you start to have interest in other people.* When others compliment you and you genuinely desire your partner's attention and affection, it is easy to entertain the idea of just

being with someone else. You may want your partner to do certain things to make you feel desired in the relationship, or that you're valuable to them, or special. If you can resist the urge to go all the way to cheater status, do it. The entanglement is not worth all the drama. However, when we're not pouring out love and affection on each other, why stay and be unhappy just because neither one of you want to let it go. When you've become invisible to each other, you might as well leave.

8. *When a relationship feels forced* is another indication that it's time to call it quits.
9. *When you feel like the trust is gone.* If you have been betrayed, or if you were the betrayer, it is a challenge to reestablish trust. It takes time, effort, and commitment beyond what's required in a normal relationship to mend something that has been broken. Without trust, there is no relationship. A lack of trust only puts stress and tension on a relationship. A lack of trust sets us up to be watched closely, wrongfully accused, and could make the salty, insecure person controlling.
10. *If they start to make you feel like nobody else wants you, or that you're not worthy of them.* That's when things start to become toxic. When they use their words to tear you down instead of building you up, know that you deserve better, and move on.
11. *When you don't feel free to be yourself,* and you're always walking on eggshells. You don't want to say the wrong thing or you feel pressured to assure them that they have all your attention all the time. Get your life!
12. *When you no longer want to be intimate with the person.* If your face is buried and your thoughts are like, *damn, hurry*

up and get this nut, it may be the end. I'm not saying that we should all want to have sex every time our partner is ready, but if you don't have moments where you look forward to the 'D', you just might be done-done.

13. *When you love the person, but you're not in love with the person.* If you have been with a person for a certain period of time, and you don't see that person as marriage material—a person that you can really spend the rest of your life with—it's time for you to walk away. Life is short, and we can waste a lot of years trying to make a person be who we want them to be. That's unfair. If you cannot allow them to be themselves, they may not be the one for you.

14. *You don't know or recognize the person you've become.* Even if you make a few adjustments in your relationship, never compromise who you are. You shouldn't leave a situation with no memory of who you were before you two met. I get it; being in a relationship means less time with your friends, but don't cut them off or burn those bridges because you have a new boo. Continue to cultivate positive friendships outside of your relationship. The right person will not only respect it—but will also encourage it.

15. *When you're poorly represented by your partner.* When you two are apart, no matter where you are, you are representations of each other. There should be no stress if you're both loyal. If you ever hear someone pull up with the line, "Aw man, I didn't know you had a girl," you might want to wonder why. Everyone is entitled to respect in relationships, in or out of their partner's presence. Sometimes the best way to teach someone to respect you is when you respect yourself first and leave their ass.

Leveling Up Starts with Loving Self

They say that if you don't sacrifice for what you want, what you want becomes the sacrifice. One of the biggest sacrifices a person can make is staying in a relationship way beyond its expiration date. If you are like many young women and want to be married with kids, holding onto a relationship longer than you should is not the best idea. Hopefully, you don't get to the point that you regret not leaving long before to start your family with a man you love, respect, and in whom you could put all your trust. Don't let your own uncertainties and lack of confidence in the future cause you to not choose to have a healthy family relationship.

Also, understand that childhood experiences impact how you view and operate in relationships. Growing up with just my mom, I didn't experience family-oriented activities like small talk about my day at the dinner table or weekend outings. There was Christmas and Thanksgiving when extended family visited, they would soon leave, and it was just me and my mom. There was nothing that I could do to get them to stay. They all had lives; and it wasn't their fault that my curiosity about "normal" or "traditional" family experiences would remain void. I accepted that it was as good as it would get.

I became content with the relationships that were offered to me in earlier years and did not force anyone to look at me in a serious manner. For a long time, marriage wasn't a thought because I had no examples of wedded bliss. It wasn't initially a goal. It wasn't something that I even knew I should obtain. I never learned what it means to support a husband, or care for him without wavering. A part of me was probably a little fearful to fuck it up, but I knew that if I jumped off into the deep end, that it would be with someone I knew would catch me and would be worth the risk.

The only solid relationships I knew were friendship that I had with my girlfriends. The love and trust in those relationships were established by how down you were to ride for each other. For instance, if something was to pop off, that is the time to prove whether or not you're a real friend. If I get into a fight, do you jump in with me? If not, you are probably not my friend. As you can tell, that wasn't sufficient enough to build the confidence to be somebody's wife. I admit, I wasn't ready for a very long time.

Obviously, it's not about fights anymore. As we mature, we learn to use our relationships to track our growth and create new desires and preferences. How could you know what you want without also knowing what you don't want? And you don't need a slew of men to test drive. Think about it. Supportive friends really have your best interests at heart without any ulterior motive. So, in that friendship, you cultivate love, trust, respect, and honesty—all traits that can carry over into romantic relationships. See, I wasn't left completely empty-handed in the "learning to be in a relationship" department. It just didn't come from my family, and my learning curve was long as fuck.

True friends see you in your most vulnerable moments. This is where we should practice the concept of love and support to apply in romantic connections. Listen: relationships are relationships. They all require honest communication, respect, and very real boundaries. Despite what we see on reality television, real friends are loyal and consistent, and wouldn't gossip about you. Another important fact is that they value what you value. They want to see you win just as much as you desire to win. Doesn't this all sound like the makings of a good romantic relationship as well? So, what I lacked in family dynamics and experience, I made up for through beautiful friendships.

Take Inventory of Yourself

I'm not perfect. If I had to admit to a flaw I've made incredible strides to overcome, it would be selfishness. Okay, don't judge me. You already know I was an only child with no real responsibilities, so the mindset I developed in childhood remained with me…for a while. When you're not used to thinking of anyone but yourself, it can come across as very selfish. It's almost as if you're constantly taking and have little to give. I had to learn reciprocation and to prioritize other people's needs, which is important for any relationship. I won't say that I always succeeded, but I knew it would need to be addressed for harmony in my relationships.

My most recent relationship probably taught me the most valuable lessons on sacrifice. My ex has a son and I was able to witness the many sacrifices a father would make for someone he loved wholeheartedly. It wasn't the same for me. My level of known sacrifice was different from his, so it was often a problem.

A second characteristic that I intentionally changed to become a better partner in my relationships was learning to properly resolve conflict. It's no secret; I was *ratchet*. The turn-up was real on a regular basis, but meeting anger with anger didn't get me anywhere; and meeting frustration with frustration only made the situation worse over time.

There was one relationship that totally made me lose my cool—and in church of all places. I almost went for blows with my supposed boyfriend over his new celebrity girlfriend. I guess I just missed the memo that we were no longer an item until that day.

The situation taught me patience. I learned to understand that people are not like me, don't think like me, and that it's not always about my perspective. Coming out of the ashes of selfish-only-child syndrome, I discovered that other people's perspectives should always be considered. A decent human being would respect other people's thoughts and allow others to feel how they feel. Just because I may not agree, doesn't mean that they're not entitled to feel how they feel. For a long time, if someone didn't agree with me, they were absolutely wrong in my book, or I saw it as a personal attack. I was forced to learn the hard truth about myself.

There was nothing anyone could tell me about me. Someone's rightful observations was perceived as bad-mouthing me, and I would shut it down—quick. I didn't take the time to listen and receive constructive criticism. This behavior bled into my adult relationships, and I knew that I had to check it.

Why am I sharing the not-so-pretty truths about myself? Because to grow we must all first identify our starting place and set an intention to get better. I discuss my flaws and areas for improvement because it's unattractive to lie to yourself. While you're reading this, you should be jogging your memory of the foul shit you've said or done and later regretted. Yeah, that. You can say you won't do it anymore, but until you get to the root of why you are the way you are and make a valid effort to change, you won't.

Understand that taking the time to get to know yourself or to work on yourself is a great reason to remain single. Don't let anyone tell you otherwise. Fall totally in love with yourself. Be completely happy with yourself. Be a light when you walk into a room, and that inner glow can only come from the love that you give yourself.

Among this list of reasons to be alone for a season are:
1. If you're still holding on to things that happened in the past.
2. If you still have trust issues.
3. If you still have traumas to overcome.

4. If you're not 100% happy with who you are by yourself. I'm going to elaborate here a bit if you don't mind. Don't look for someone else to complete you. If you need them to be happy you are creating a co-dependent relationship that is detrimental to your well-being.

I couldn't become the woman that I am by myself. Mentors offered positive examples and helped me to set goals. They taught me that if I want something for myself, to be ambitious in the pursuit of it. Trying to conquer this thing called life alone may not have been impossible, but it was made easier with the support of those who nurtured me and wanted to see me win. Not only that, but they also became a trusted source to identify and address my personal shortcomings. There must be someone in your corner to guide you, whether it's a relationship you develop with someone from your church or a counselor.

Let's Talk About Sex, Baby

What do you believe makes up a healthy sexual relationship? People tend to view sex from the lens of sexual traumas and really don't know what is healthy, or what they truly want in the bedroom. Sex is merely entertainment for some, and they're entitled to that. If you're into the multiple-partner acts, just be safe and fully understand your *why* before you engage. My greatest concern is that women feel respected. Despite your sexual appetite, or lack thereof, a woman should feel comfortable enough to let someone in, and not feel pressured by a man or any societal standards. These days, there are a plethora of twerk classes, pole dancing classes, penis sucking classes, and "D" riding classes (yes, that's a thing…look it up), as women feel empowered to improve their sexual delivery. I'm only against it if a woman feels pressured to partake in these activities for the sake of just keeping a man. Boo, a man who wants to be kept will be kept. There are some chicks out here with good sex game that are still lied to and cheated on. A man must respect the whole of you, and not just be satisfied with what you do in the bedroom—although it helps.

I grew up accepting the Bible's definition of marriage as the standard and understood that there should be one husband and one wife; but with the influx of polyamorous relationships, it's obvious that times have changed. Again, if you're led to lifestyles that deviate from tradition, get to a place of fully understanding how those relationship dynamics speak to you and fulfills your desires. Don't do it because it's a trend, and never enter a lifestyle solely because your partner wants it.

Women are, and have always been, viewed differently than men. It's no secret. We're easily judged as whores and sluts when we own our sexuality and display more than what society is accustomed to seeing. This stigma developed from the expectation for us to be classy individuals with one partner. You know…respectable. Meanwhile, the men seem able to say, do, and screw anything they'd like and it's acceptable. I'm not saying that women should take those same liberties but should take ownership of their own bodies—which is sacred—and know your worth.

The Universal "Hell No!"

Some people don't know when to walk away from a dying relationship in hopes that it could be revived. Let me say this: if the relationship is abusive, it is best that you leave to save yourself than to hope for the moment things change, or "dead" won't just be a word to describe your relationship. Harsh, I know. Bold, I know—

but it's true. And I want you to live. Death by domestic violence hits close to home—real close.

Taffi was my cousin—and you know how Blacks from the south are about cousins. She divorced my first cousin and they'd had a son together before she started dating someone else. He was very ambitious, a firefighter; but she wouldn't know how many fires he would start in her life.

He was abusive, but she kept it a secret for a long time. She had been warned by people who'd heard stories about him to just walk away. So, to avoid the "I told you so," she refused to talk about it. When she finally decided to open up to a friend, she explained that if something was to ever happen to her, that it was him; and she gave her instructions on how to care for her young son. She was getting things in order because she sensed that his threat was real. After breaking her arm, along with other shit around the house, she knew that his severe aggression couldn't be contained. Even after receiving a restraining order, she still didn't feel safe. The document only covered South Haven, Mississippi, and not Memphis, Tennessee, where she was employed as a nurse.

One morning, he borrowed a neighbor's car and followed her. As soon as she stepped foot out of the car, he started firing his gun. He even stood over her and continued to shoot before he fled the scene. Taffi died that day.

We later discovered that his abuse wasn't new. He had done the same thing to his ex-wife, but her father was a pastor and she spoke up about it, which saved her. They hid her from him. Taffi had just stayed in the relationship far too long and didn't let anyone in until it was too late. No one was there to protect her because she refused to let anyone in.

Abuse is never okay—physical, emotional, verbal. That's not love. Love shouldn't hurt. It doesn't hurt. It shouldn't make you feel like you must sacrifice to be a strong person and endure it. That is not included in "for better for worse." That's bullshit right there. You must know when to get out, and know when to let others in. Don't worry about judgment when your life is on the line. Many women stay for their children or for financial reasons. Others stay because they suffer from damaged confidence and believe they can't survive without their abuser, which happens when they're made to feel like nothing for many years.

I knew the First Lady of a church who was in an abusive relationship with her pastor husband. Because of their status, she found it more difficult to leave him. Plus, they were saved and community leaders—she found it impossible to get out. She wanted to embody strength and resilience, but she was suffering. Women like her are prone to stay around longer than they should to make it work—until the day comes that they can just not take it anymore, or it's just too late.

My advice: if there is still breath in your body, get out while you can. If that seems impossible, at least make it a point to talk about what's happening in your relationship with a trusted person. This can both change your life—and save it.

CHAPTER EIGHT
Figuring Myself Out

It's okay to be indecisive and to try new things until you find what works, or to keep a steady vision in mind until you achieve it. As I mentioned, I didn't initially have any real direction, but I held the idea that I would someday own a company and have multiple people working for me. However, I was looking for something that would fulfill me right away. Atlanta opened my eyes to so many opportunities that I never knew existed, and I tried to figure out where I fit in. I wished there was someone who was already who could guide me through the process. And although I would do research to understand and land the job, I should have had a plan. Fortunately, I never ended up on the street, or in an enormous amount of debt from tuition trying to learn everything.

At one point, I saw a market for graphic design, and because of my technology background, I accumulated some side gigs building websites. That led to designing billboards and flyers and other kinds of marketing materials. I even enrolled in college to study art and design to take that interest to the next level. I attended graphic design school my first year in Atlanta, and the two-year program initiated my journey in graphic design.

After design school, I interned at a small company that was a force in the marketing business. Mark Starr Media was the hub for the big name rappers, artists, and singers. Keep in mind that it was back in the day when people still handed out paper flyers to promote upcoming events, and the company had celebrity clientele that always needed materials, or billboards. I interned there for about three years before I started my own business, B Platinum Graphics.

I started taking on my own graphic gigs. I was doing flyers, websites, menus, and logos. Name any type of company marketing and branding, and I did it. It was hard work, but it everything was working out. Designing websites took a lot of time because I was building webpages from scratch. Web design in those days was not how it is now—where you can just design a website with a drag and drop builder or premade templates. I was writing with code the old-fashioned way. I found that I was spending a lot of late nights at the computer more often than was beneficial to me, my work-life balance, and my health. Eventually, I slowed down on building web pages, but I continued to do graphics.

There was a season when I worked in mortgages for Wells Fargo, but I learned the business wasn't for me. Training later became my full-time gig but, in addition to working long hours at the gym, I worked with IBM as a supplemental employee. The relationship with IBM was formed when I was tapped by a recruiter to do a computer system job as a one-off. Some of the others who worked on that project were with IBM. I always had the gift of gab when I needed it, so I asked how I could get on with IBM. They told me where to send my resume and a few months later I was called by IBM. I worked on projects a few times a week, often overnight, and would lead a system refresh at a major retailer like Best Buy. I would program their servers, computers, and database, or install POS systems. The shift would start at nine, and I wouldn't leave until the next morning. We also did projects for Hilton Hotels, and I was usually the lead tech on these projects.

Despite these roles and the skills I cultivated over time, I never knew how much I would love fitness, but it became my passion. I was always a natural at fitness. If you're like most people, you understand that you just get tired of things after a while. I got tired of the mortgage business. I got tired of competitions. With any job I held, I got tired of it. It was no longer fulfilling even though I couldn't say why. Helping people, and my desire to build a family and a community of like-minded people, was just so natural. It was what I wanted to do.

As I continued my own training regimen, I was also focused on building my clientele, which included multiple celebrity clients. I started to train competitors and focused on the mental health of my clients. As a result, I learned that many people just didn't love themselves. They could have an amazing body, but their mental health was below par. Their past hiccups hindered them from genuine happiness. Some clients were in bad marriages, abusive relationships, or bad financial situations. As they went through their roughest seasons, they would come to the gym as an outlet, but were inconsistent because of what they dealt with internally. We would converse, and I'd offer my advice when asked, but it made me realize that there was more to health and fitness than what meets the eye.

I trained clients from five in the morning until nine at night, and believed I had a real business going. It was detrimental in some ways because I had no understanding of a good work-life balance and had compromised family time and personal relationships. I even sacrificed attending my stepson's games. Although he had other family there, my failure to support him brought up my own childhood experiences when my parents were absent. I understood the pain I could cause, but I consistently put my clients first. I was never okay with it, but I assumed that I was doing the right thing by staying focused.

Even after building a good base of celebrity clientele, and my ability to help trainers with graphics and marketing materials, I still felt that there was still more to do. My full transition into personal training is what led me to massage therapy.

I attended massage therapy school every day for nine months. Although I received financial aid, there were a lot of out-of-pocket expenses leftover. Enrollment was a real sacrifice because I still wasn't making an abundance of money. I did whatever was necessary to finish the course, and knew that when I finished, I would be an amazing massage therapist. While I was in school, clients who came in for a massage offered great feedback on my work. It was in those moments that I was confident I was on the road to completing the full package of services I could provide as a personal trainer. I knew I had so much to offer.

Adding massage therapy to my portfolio must not have been in the cards. This may come as a shock, but I ended my pursuit of certification in massage therapy because I did not like the idea of touching people's bodies. You must understand that not all bodily fluids or hair growth is created equal, and people come with all sorts of ailments and conditions that therapists must overlook to perform the task. As a result, I tried to start my own massage business and outsource employees to do massages. This plan also fell through when I became nervous about liability and feared what would happen if I sent an employee into stranger's house who had ill-intent. Don't fret. I count none of these moments as failures, but lessons along the path, and soon after, I was in the military full-time and deployed to the Middle East.

An Unexpected Quest for Inspiration

When you are in the process of looking for what you want to do in life, traveling outside of your environment can be helpful. It can open your eyes to new ways of doing things or put your own life and its challenges into perspective. While I discussed the hardships of being deployed to the Middle East in the previous chapter, I would be remiss if I didn't also reveal the beautiful moments that unfolded while I was there. During the eight-month tour, my time in Qatar and Kuwait was particularly eye-opening. I met a lot of good people as well as people I couldn't wait to forget. Outside of the base, life is very different from what we experience here in the United States.

The culture seemed very male-centric. Women had to stay fully clothed with a burqa and could only show their eyes. Marriages were arranged. A woman was not supposed to speak if a man was in the room. If you lived on the base and had to go off-base to take your daughter to the ER, you could not go in the room with her. You had to be married to check into a hotel as a couple. I understand that some of these rules are meant to facilitate modesty, but some of them struck me as taking respect away from women.

Women don't seem to have very many rights. At that time, they were not allowed to drive, or even look up when someone was speaking to them. Men were allowed to have multiple wives if they could care for them. A man's first wife is supposed to be his spouse for having children and building a family. The second wife can be a more romantic interest. The third wife is typically a widow without children. They have a whole system worked out, but it seemed as if women are there for procreation or enjoyment in some ways they're treated like property.

I had grown up experiencing segregation myself, and this was a reminder of that, even if it's part of their culture. Seeing life like this in the Middle East did not make me dismiss my own personal experience, but it made me see that everybody and every group has its struggles. I never really felt the need to change anything about it all, because it's a different mentality; I just wouldn't want to live in a place like that. I did share my thoughts on this with a friend I had made there when I asked her if she ever considered leaving the Middle East. I learned it's not that easy. We did our best to respect the culture of the people around the base. We could not touch people of the opposite gender, per their religious beliefs. Ramadan was tough, and we could not eat or drink in front of any locals if they were working on the base or at the gates.

The Middle East is also rich. Some of the people in these countries are very wealthy; there is so much generational wealth. The driving there is very different. It's overly aggressive and we would perceive some of the drivers as disrespectful. They will run you off the road if you're not careful. If they crash a car, they'll park it and go buy another one. Wealth in countries like Qatar and Kuwait has made beautiful cities with skyscrapers and constant construction.

Many assume that being military means you travel a lot, or that those who join the military like to travel. I was open to the idea of traveling but was initially scared to go overseas. When I completed a tour of duty in the Middle East, I realized how much we learn when we travel, even if it's just around America. There is so much more to the world than where I grew up and becoming aware of this has increased my eagerness to learn more. I've seen things I've learned about in history really brought them to life.

In school, history was not my favorite subject because it was so far removed from my life. Seeing the actual locations of, say, the Civil Rights movement—standing in those places and thinking about the struggles the people endured—made it real. Standing in the Lorraine Hotel where Martin Luther King, Jr. was assassinated, visiting the sites of the Underground Railroad, crossing the bridge at Selma, Alabama can send chills down your spine. It's sad that growing up I didn't really understand the story of the struggle to end slavery or the resilient push of the Civil Rights Movement but stepping into the past made me want to live my own life to the fullest and ensure others would not be mistreated. This was part of the reason I became an EO.

As I mentioned in the previous chapter, my Middle East tour brought up some mental health challenges. I had to put in some work to get myself back to an emotionally healthy place. I took the recommendations that were given to me in therapy to deal with the PTSD that stemmed from deployment, but it also caused me to reset and rethink what I wanted to do next. I bounced around several places to find my professional path until I realized I had to slow down and put things in order. I finally started to think about birthing my own business—not just personal training, and definitely not working in a corporate setting for someone else's dream. Working overseas inspired my pursuit of independence and the desire to fully exercise our American liberties, including a woman's ability to build her own empire.

Realigning Passion

Although I was passionate and loved my clients, personal training had not moved me to where I wanted to be. I was physically tired. Fitness was where I wanted to be, but I desired to expand and take on other projects that were related to it. Discovering new ways to generate revenue and success through my work without being overworked was important and it became an imminent goal to have part of my revenue work *for me* without any physical labor. Balancing my work life and personal life became a priority for me, and I figured it could only help to have a business that I could run from home.

The idea to start an apparel company sprung from my ex, who had an aspiration to have his own clothing line. Initially, I was hesitant. It was new territory for me, and I was far from ready. Sometimes you just aren't ready for an idea until you're ready. Once I figured out what I needed to do to start the clothing line, I went all in and never looked back. With my background in graphic design, I could take care of that part myself. So, I designed all my pieces, with the help of my friend who taught me graphic design when I was an intern. I wanted my clothing to be different from what everyone else offered. I wanted the designs to be my own so that no one could go online and find them without looking specifically for me.

Inventory would be a hassle because of how much I travel with the military, but I found a company that allows me to create my own designs and will print each item as they are ordered by customers. This is the drop shipping model.

When you come up with an idea, write it down no matter how crazy it sounds. Figure out how you can make it work for you. I knew how everyone else had started a clothing line: getting shipments from overseas, sending out inventory, etc. That was the most lucrative way to do it since bulk purchasing meant more profit. As someone who couldn't store the inventory, I would have to pay for items one at a time, and essentially trade profit for convenience I couldn't do without.

I focused on the long run of building a brand and not just placing items with my name on it in stores. My new business partner and I had interned together during my graphic design career, and he played a prominent part on the backend to get the business off the ground. Believe me, there were tons of obstacles, and no future entrepreneur should think it will be easy. There were times when I felt exhausted and was overworking myself. It didn't feel like I was getting anywhere. I was investing more and more time but was not making more money; I was stressed and didn't believe it would work. It's going to be stressful and anything that could happen is probably going to happen; but you must have a mindset to figure it out and stay the course. Keep going until you find something that works to fix the problems you encounter. You can't give up.

That was my mindset when I went into it. My clothing line was launched in December 2018. The brand had a lot of good feedback and I perfected the mission behind the brand, which gave it some momentum. At this point, my brand continues to evolve because I discover ways to improve my brand every day.

Branding is a journey, and not a destination. A major part of building a brand is investing time and money and being consistent until it hits. At the time I'm writing this book, for example, I'm still in the military full time. The second I leave work, I go home to sit at the computer for hours and hours and hours—sometimes until two or three in the morning—working on my product designs and ensuring I communicate with my customers. Well…first I work out, and then maybe get something to eat, but by five or six in the evening I'm ensconced at the computer.

A big part of business is marketing. Marketing is vital to the success and endurance of any business. In my first year after hiring a publicist, my brand was featured on *Good Morning America*, and I landed a project with Burt's Bees, a subsidiary of Clorox. They came in and filmed a short documentary which was featured on the *Herstory* online series. I've been featured in magazines and blogs, and I'm regularly scheduled for photoshoots. My products and merchandise to are submitted to influencers, which is the current trend to increase product recognition. Some just love to follow stylish, popular people who could have a paper sack over their head and still sell whatever they're wearing just from a simple social media post. However, you've got to put in work to connect with these people and get them on your side to spread the message; when you're in business for yourself, you should never omit a potential avenue to success.

Discovering Purpose and Authenticity

As detailed in this chapter, I wandered through several potential career paths as I took the journey to figure myself out: mortgages, graphic design, information systems and computer engineering, the military, personal training. Ultimately, each of these experiences would contribute to the idea I've finally birthed: my coaching business and my brand. The military provided discipline and focus. The mortgage business taught me about personal finance. Computer engineering taught me how to build and run a website. Graphic design helped me to design a unique product line and market it. Personal training helped me to understand why people engage in exercise and how to properly help them get healthy. Now, my brand is evolving and expanding into new territories. I offer supplements and workout equipment in addition to the fitness apparel. It has blossomed fully into a brand now, and part of it is the amazing coaching program I will discuss later.

Before we go there, let's take a moment to reflect. Think about how you most enjoy spending your day. What are you doing? Are you creating something? Working with your hands? Solving life's problems? Counseling a friend? Working out? Now consider how you can do that thing and assist others in some way. Life is all about helping others—to achieve something, to attain something, to understand something. Some of the wealthiest people in the world own inventions that resulted from their desire to solve a problem other people were having. What problem can you help to solve?

What is unique about what you have to offer? Therein lies your purpose.

If you think anything going to be handed to you then you are in for a rude awakening. The best ability is availability. That means showing up for yourself the way you show up for someone else's business or corporation. The key to success is consistency. Consistency establishes your reputation. Success doesn't come from what you do occasionally, it comes from what you do consistently; and trust and believe that people are watching. If you believe in something hard enough, your day will eventually come. I'd be a fool to tell you that there won't be any trials and tribulations, but your purpose and your *why* must be stronger and bigger than you. You are unstoppable when you simply trust and believe in yourself.

It's totally fine if you're like I was and move from place to place on a quest to discover your true purpose in this world, but it is possible that you're simply running from it. They say that when you're in alignment with what you're created to do, work just doesn't feel like work. Perhaps it is the very thing that you love to do most that, if you just focus your attention and gather information, can not only be fulfilling but lucrative as well. Make no apologies for what you discover on this leg of your journey and allow the steps to naturally unfold. You can't force it if you tried, but you must surrender to the process of having all that you can ever imagine.

The BRAND
8 Figured Body

We spend so much of our lives dedicated to the success of other people. The truth is that you can be your own boss and invest that energy into your own success. In this chapter, I want you to discover one of the best parts of my brand: my coaching program.

Throughout the years, my style of coaching separated me from other coaches because of my background in health and wellness. I've coached in this arena for almost 17 years have created an organized program that goes for six weeks and includes personalized meal plans fitness routines. Each group is capped at a certain number, so I expect full commitment from those who are selected.

At this point, the entire program is virtual; and we engage daily in our group chats. However, there is nothing remote about the participation. We meet virtually each week for mental health checks. Although there are no virtual workouts, this method is better than personal training. With personal training, clients would come to the gym and then you home; and I don't see them until the next time we meet. With the program, I'm involved every day, and actively help participants to reach their goals. There is more accountability from me and from the group as whole, as they have the tendency to check in on each other.

When it comes to issuing meal plans and workout plans, it is imperative that you are under the direction of a professional personal trainer. I'm very careful with creating personalized plans and will observe participants as they work through them. The program just doesn't work if you sign up and you don't work out, or if you're still eating whatever you want because there are no eyes on you. That's why I prefer to instill real change with the program than to simply offer a meal or exercise plan.

The program started out as something that I wanted to do for my hometown of Winona, Mississippi. My first event was on Thanksgiving in 2014 when I hosted a three-day wellness program. I also discussed health and fitness and answered questions. I was moved to help my city because people were steadily passing away from heart disease, strokes, and obesity at very young ages. There was not a lot of consistent physical activity. There was little understanding of what eating right looked like. It was an opportunity to give back to my hometown.

Afterwards, I started to develop online health challenges. *Can you run 100 miles in 30 days? Can you go 21 days without bread or sweets?* Many people signed up and were motivated, which indicated that there was some interest there. I said to myself, *Let me do a six-week challenge and see how that works out.*

Something was developing, but I didn't know how it would turn out. I started to believe that I could have more impact if participants were under my direction instead of having periodic coaching moments, and this was the start of my transition into coaching. Initially, I offered the program for no charge because I didn't know where it was going. People signed up, but since they weren't paying, they acted as if it was something they did or didn't have to do. To them, it was no big deal either way. They weren't invested in the program, or into themselves really.

I saw that giving the program away for free wasn't working. I wasn't reaching them. So, I decided to add a commitment fee, although it was still nowhere near what it's worth. I still started to have better results. When people pay for something, they are invested and will put more work into it, especially in Mississippi where money is hard to come by and investing in health is a serious commitment. They started to take it more seriously. Charging for the program didn't drive people away; it brought them in. I started to get more and more groups of people who took it seriously. By the end of the year, hundreds of people had reached out and wanted to be in program, but it was still dirt cheap. The value of this program is easily more than premium-price worthy, but I was charging almost pennies.

It was draining me. People weren't paying me for my time, and I had put hours and hours into it. The truth of the matter is that it was not about profit, but about helping people. That was the drive then, and it is now. I just wanted people to be able to afford it.

The program had blossomed into something unexpected. Back then, it was called *The 6-Week Beast Mode Challenge*, but it sounded a little too transitory, like a one-off event. Now it's *The 8Figure Body*, which is part of my 8Figured brand. The program is about changing your entire outlook on life—which is reflected in the name of the program. The number 8 might make you think of an hourglass shape or a dollar sign, but that's not the endgame of getting fit in our community. I'm challenging you to turn that 8 on its side and see it as the sign for infinity—to recognize the infinite possibilities presented to each of us in health and wellness—mentally, physically, emotionally, spiritually, and financially. There is no greater wealth than health; and you can't be wealthy without your health.

8Figured represents an abundance of joy, love, and total satisfaction with yourself. I aim to teach you to discard negative self-talk and move past body preoccupations for improved mental and physical health—to a more fulfilling life. True beauty flows from the confidence within the individual, and I strive to help you develop a positive relationship with your body while raising your self-esteem. This is more than a fitness brand; it's a lifestyle of accepting ourselves and being good stewards of the priceless bodies we were given. And that's where the fitness program ties into the clothing line. People in the world of health and fitness express themselves with their attire. I design clothing that celebrates the wearer's individuality—but also their participation in a community that inspires and empowers. All sizes and shapes can feel good working out in my apparel. If someone suffers with poor body image or depression, I also want them to feel good in my apparel.

The first part of *The 8Figure Body* program is a consultation. That's when I select those who can join the program because I don't allow just anyone to participate. You must be approved. I have turned people away because they were not ready. Sometimes when people go through major life events they are not able to be plugged into something like this. I'll coach you through those moments when life happens, but I try to get people to be realistic. If you've recently experienced a major life event, there are many things you can do to be a healthier you, but this program is intense, and won't do anything but stress you out if you already have a lot going on. I look for those who want to do this and who can commit.

People cry on the initial call. They get emotional when they realize how they let themselves get to the point of obesity, insecurity, or self-hate. When going through tough times, a lot of people bury themselves in sorrow. Some eat their pain away or just let themselves go to the point where they don't even like to look in the mirror anymore. Of course, the calls are confidential. People in the program may know each other, so I never discuss or disclose anything that is said. I simply recognized the powerful benefit of consultation calls and the relief the participants felt as they shared with me, and that's when I knew this program would move participants beyond physical transformations and would help transform their lives. I was ready to show them how to get themselves back.

I tell people that the program is 80% mental effort. That's the first thing to overcome because there is no health without mental health. You can't even begin to think about eating right or exercising if you're not in a mentally healthy position, not in a good environment, or if you're surrounded by bad influences, which were some of my own challenges. Many times, in fact, I tell participants how much I can relate to their challenges.

You need to become aware of these areas and make changes, if needed, to be successful. And that's why the program is so amazing; it forces you to not only confront the physical you, but the internal you as well—the things many people think they need to suppress. Here's news: they can't be suppressed and must be worked out.

Next comes the personalized meal plan. I send a questionnaire to participants because everybody is different. They typically have different goals. Some might want to lose weight or gain weight, which means they would consume entirely different foods. Then there might be some things you can't eat; or you might have a specific diet that is vegan or pescatarian. You might not like chicken or you can't eat pork. Each meal plan is tailored to you and whatever your goals are. You can't just give someone a cookie cutter meal plan if they have specific goals. I write out each one and provide a grocery list.

I also include additional protein options, because one day you might not want chicken, and you want salmon. It helps make sure participants don't get bored. *The 8Figure Body* is about creating a lifestyle, not a restrictive diet. I don't believe in diets. With my program, you learn to eat for life and how to substitute some foods for healthier ones. Teaching you to calculate your map roads—how much protein, fats, and carbs you'll need throughout the day—is my way of coaching you to be self-sufficient.

My workout training plan is personalized as well. Whether you want to tone up, lose weight, gain weight, or increase cardio, workouts are tailored to you on a weekly basis. When we check in at the end of each week, I ask about your progress with the workouts and will not give you a new one until you gotten the previous workout right. I'm very involved in every aspect of this program. Being so hands on, I can choose to change it up only when we get it perfect.

Life happens. People travel out of town. There are birthday parties. Dinner parties. You might say, "I'm going to a birthday party, and we're going to X restaurant? Can you look at the menu and tell me what I can have, and what I need to request from the server?" Guess what: I do all that. How many other programs offer that level of care and commitment to bringing you into a healthy lifestyle? On the other hand, I'll tell you, honestly, that if you're going to your child's football game, you'll need to pack your lunch, because otherwise you'll be at the concession stand eating something you're not supposed to be eating.

It's important to take the diet plan seriously and stick to it. Even if you say, "Oh, I'm just going to get a hamburger," you haven't considered the seasoning and what they put in it to make it taste good. I coach and train you and offer insight that will cause you to think about what you eat. I teach you how to read labels so that you're not fooled by a piece of lettuce on the package when you see the amount of sugar or sodium or trans-fat in the product. You learn to be more aware, so if you decide to eat something, you know the effects. You can say to yourself: *I know I'm supposed to have this much sodium for the day, and haven't hit that limit yet, so this should be okay.* This method gives the meal plan some flexibility because you understand how to monitor what you're eating. It offers longevity because you'll know how to make healthier choices, and you get better at it over time.

Some people participate in the program multiple times. It's a lifestyle change, and it takes time to master what your body needs. We revisit our goals to make sure we are on the right path. We check in all the time. If you're having a bad week and you can't get a workout in, that's when it matters the most, because you are forced to find the strength to push yourself. Maybe there's stress on the job, a death in the family, or even something as simple as wanting to come home and relax after work. That's how you get into that couch mode. You must look at your schedule and plan. *I know I'm tired when I step through the door, so I must hit the fitness club at some point before I get home or find a way to snap myself out of it and just go straight to the gym.* We talk about ways to fix those barriers and we create plans that work.

I have a private group for each challenge where people can buddy up, especially if they are going through similar circumstances or have similar goals. They often check in with each other. Supporters on my crew help with accountability as well. The only way to fail at this program is if you just don't do it. Everything you'll need is at your disposal. Even if you do it halfway, you'll see amazing results because of the energy and effort that's put into making this community great.

We have Zoom workouts, and my group is called TrapStars. It's kind of a cute play on words, like Beyoncé has her Beyhive. TrapStars stems from the word "trap" which means the trapezoid muscles. We have Trap Queens, Trap Kings, and the Trap House workout, and we say we trap on Wednesday. When people fall off, we call it falling off the Trap Train. Of course, they get back on, but we have fun with it.

As of March 2022, the program is blossoming into something new and I want to attract a different type of clientele. I don't regret the pricing I had before, because over the past few years I've really changed a lot of lives. It's time for the program to step into its true worth. I'm done with the test run. I know it works. I know it's amazing. Now, I'm only looking for serious people to participate because I get them serious results. My crew is professional and certified in their respective disciplines, and there are people who completed previous challenges who are onboard to help. There are doctors, nutritionists, mental health professionals who have taken the program and stepped the game up.

Participants are in various time zones—from Hawaii to Alaska to California to New York to Germany—which was one of the advantages of going from in-person personal training to coaching. Technology allows me to branch out. People I've never met before consistently reach out to me because they heard about the program through friends or family. It's spreading all over the world, which is so amazing, and I'm so excited. The pandemic put a stamp of approval on remote learning, and people like to do things on their own time, including choosing to go to their home gym to be away from others, or choosing to go to their local gym for some interaction. It's your choice, and you can do it any time that's convenient for you.

The apparel line, products, and fitness program are all a part of the lifestyle and community I'm building. I started with just a clothing line and moved into wellness challenges. Now, I have supplements, waist trainers, gloves, and I'm expanding into other products like jump ropes. I don't know how far I will go with it, but I just grow it as I go.

A lot of great things are happening, and I'm also excited about the wellness expos I'll be starting. They are in-person, three-day events with guest speakers, celebrities, and political figures who will share their own stories of how they overcame challenges and how you can overcome yours.

A Different Type of Fire

I've been doing *The 8Figure Body* for two years now. I'm not a multimillionaire and I'm not even where I want to be, but I still consider myself a success story simply because I refuse to give up; I'm growing and hitting milestones. I see things I want to change and I evolve. I'm building a great team of people to have in my corner as we prepare to move to the next level. Some of them will become entrepreneurs themselves and are real valuable nuggets.

I barely get any sleep, although I know it doesn't sound like the healthiest thing for a coach to say. It's just a grind in me—a different type of fire that's been lit. I put so much into my brand and my business that there is no turning back. You'll get to the point where your work will be so important that you'll do whatever it takes to win. I've invested so much time working in the landscape of corporate America in places like Wells Fargo, IBM, the military, or for someone else's business, that I would be selling myself short if I didn't invest just as much into myself.

There is nothing wrong with working for someone else, mind you. Everybody is different. Not everyone is meant to be their own boss. Some people are meant to be the ones pulling the strings in the background, and we need them to push our own businesses. Some people are just great at supporting; and they're born managers and leaders on the battlefield.

I don't know if I'll go broke trying to make this thing successful, but I'm going all the way to the end and do everything I can to pour into it. Even this book is a part of building the brand and community, because I'm inviting you to travel my journey with me and discover what it took for me to get to this point despite racism, illness, PTSD, going overseas to fight for our country, and growing up in small-town Mississippi where most people believe that where you came from dictates how much success you'll have in life. Success, however, looks different to different people. For some, it's the attainment of money that equals success. For others, it's the ability to overcome challenges that indicates a person's achievements. I never want people to feel that not having an abundance of money or never reaching your goal is an indication of failure or doesn't mean anything. Success is where you came from versus where you are now, and the challenges you had to face to get here and still stand strong.

If you have thoughts of becoming an entrepreneur and birthing a project or a brand, this message is for you. If you work for a large corporation and are trying to move further on that path, this book is for you too. Whatever it is, be the best at it. If you're a fast-food worker, be the best fast-food worker you could ever be. Do whatever you can to be where you want to be. Even if you're not yet at the desired level, own it and be happy.

Success is about happiness. Whatever happiness looks like to you, that's exactly what you should chase; and you must never allow society to define success for you. Be content with being different, because if you chase the success that really matters to you, chances are you are going to be different from those around you.

I hope I encouraged you to think about where you currently are in your life as I shared my journey with you. Through this work, you have discovered my ability to I overcame family drama, segregation and racism, and even physical and mental health issues. Everybody's challenges are different—but we all have them. The question is always: how do we overcome each challenge and live our best life?

CONCLUSION
Get It, Girl

Life is hard. You'll be presented with challenges but you'll also have moments where you will see the silver lining and count your experiences for growth. Keep your head up! Know that you can get to wherever you desire to be, and that you can achieve whatever you want if you consistently make strides towards it. Remove the stumbling blocks. Go above and beyond. Face your fears. Keep the faith!

Don't allow anything or anybody to stop you from being who you want to be. Even if people look at you and laugh, keep going and never lose hope. Don't allow other people's negativity to become internalized negative self-talk. You're smart enough. You have the right tools it takes to get to the top.

Be mindful of the people you keep in your corner. Those who truly love you will never stop, but first loving yourself makes you a magnet for the genuine love of others.

Pray every day and allow God to guide you. When things get tough and appear as if it won't work out, don't get frustrated and throw in the towel. The toughest times created some of the best lessons for me, and they can do the same for you. Look for a lesson in every situation that you encounter. If God puts it on your path, know that there is a reason for it. It's so cliche but it's so true.

No matter what, keep going and never give up. You have a purpose in life, so everything that you do must have purpose. Allow every action that you take to drive you closer to fulfilling that purpose.

At the end of the day, love every aspect of **you**. Challenge yourself to be better each day. Set an intention to wake up better than you were the day before.

Continue to educate yourself. Growing up in Mississippi as a Black woman, I had many strikes against me. The key to my success was the education they didn't want us to have. Even in the military, I had to prove myself valuable. It's not easy to move up the ranks in a White man's world without respect and being undervalued. That is why I tell you to value yourself and know your worth. Otherwise, people will treat you based on the value they assign to you even when you're worth so much more.

Know when to let go, when to disconnect from things and people along your path that don't mean you any good. You're going to lose a lot of people. Accept that and be okay. Everyone is not meant to go where you're going.

Do not be ashamed of who you are and where you came from but strive to be the best person you can be. Be authentic and be the best version of yourself. Do good and good will come to you.

Wishing you all the best.

"When it comes to the past, we can never run away. We must either confront it or let it go —which isn't the same as running away."

THE FIGHT: To Build Resilience

Some of the ways that I felt uncared for as a child were...

_____
_____
_____
_____
_____

It is possible that the adversities of my childhood impact my current relationships or the way I see the world in this way...

_____
_____
_____
_____
_____

THE FIGHT: To Build Resilience

What are some good memories from childhood? Are these memories a safe space for me to go to when I'm scared or upset?

_____
_____
_____
_____
_____

How have I tried to avoid repeating certain aspects of childhood in my adult life with my own children or with myself?

_____
_____
_____
_____
_____

THE FIGHT: To Build Resilience

Taking an honest look at my own life, am I repeating any patterns that I hoped I wouldn't?

_____

_____

_____

_____

_____

What events from my past continue to haunt me? Have I properly forgiven those who created deep pain? How can I forgive myself for allowing the pain to linger for so long?

_____

_____

_____

_____

_____

"Whenever I receive a blessing or achieve success, I am more grateful because I can compare my accomplishments to previous lack and failures."

THE FIGHT: To Build Resilience

I would describe my childhood environment as...

_____
_____
_____
_____
_____

This environment contributed to my success in life by...

_____
_____
_____
_____
_____

THE FIGHT: To Build Resilience

This environment held me back from success by...

_____
_____
_____
_____
_____

How did the way I grow up shape my worldview? My relationships?

_____
_____
_____
_____
_____

THE FIGHT: To Build Resilience

It what ways might I show up as small-minded, inflexible, or fearful?

_____
_____
_____
_____
_____

What practices will assist in reversing childhood programming that hinders me from achieving great peace, success or having healthy relationships?

_____
_____
_____
_____
_____

"It was up to me to remove the blinders and pursue a lifestyle that was in alignment with the vision of success I had developed for myself."

THE FIGHT: To Build Resilience

The 5 people I spend the most time with are...

_____

_____

_____

_____

_____

My closest friends have these goals in life...

_____

_____

_____

_____

_____

THE FIGHT: To Build Resilience

My closest friends encourage me by...

_____
_____
_____
_____
_____

Those who discourage me the most tend to say things like...

_____
_____
_____
_____
_____

THE FIGHT: To Build Resilience

Some positive attributes that my friends possess are...

_____

_____

_____

_____

_____

Being honest with myself, am I easily led by others or do I blaze my own trail? How am I **negatively** influenced by those around me?

_____

_____

_____

_____

_____

"When you recognize that you're off course, jump back on! It's not going to be an easy path."

THE FIGHT: To Build Resilience

When I am at a crossroads or potential turning point in my life, how do I make decisions ? How are my decisions influenced by other people?

_____
_____
_____
_____
_____

How can I make my own decisions while still respecting the wishes of people who love me?

_____
_____
_____
_____
_____

THE FIGHT: To Build Resilience

Historically, what have been some indicators that it is time to transition to a new place or a new level? How can you better identify these moments?

_____

_____

_____

_____

_____

Do I have a history of taking risks and trying new things? In what ways can I stop simply resorting to safety and lingering in the familiar?

_____

_____

_____

_____

_____

THE FIGHT:
To Build Resilience

How can I set myself up for success when I leave structured environments to make it on my own?

_____
_____
_____
_____
_____

How do I know if a certain path isn't right for me? What are some clues that I receive that I am moving in the right direction?

_____
_____
_____
_____
_____

THE FIGHT: To Build Resilience

Based on past experiences, what are ways that I can tell opportunity is knocking? How can I open myself up to see more opportunities?

_____
_____
_____
_____
_____

How can I channel my innate character traits or my past in a healthy way?

_____
_____
_____
_____
_____

"It was my job. It was what I had to do; but it started to affect me. I was numb to it at the time because I was one of the few in charge, and I knew the job had to be done."

THE FIGHT: To Build Resilience

How have I dealt with them physical and mental health challenges? How can I better address them in the future?

_____
_____
_____
_____
_____

Am I willing to accept help for physical and mental health issues? If I'm not, what is holding me back from accepting that help?

_____
_____
_____
_____
_____

"When you come up with an idea, write it down no matter how crazy it sounds. Figure out how you can make it work for you."

THE FIGHT: To Build Resilience

What did my childhood-self want to be when I grew up? What exactly did I assume I would do after graduating college? Is that still my desire? If not, how has it changed?

_____
_____
_____
_____
_____

What things **don't** I get tired of? What activities am I consistently passionate about?

_____
_____
_____
_____
_____

THE FIGHT: To Build Resilience

How have the different stopping points along my professional journey contributed to where I am now? How might they contribute to something in the future?

_____
_____
_____
_____
_____

Have I ever taken a moment to rest, reset, and rethink my goals and career path? Do I need to take that kind of moment now?

_____
_____
_____
_____
_____

"Success is about happiness. Whatever happiness looks like to you, that's exactly what you should chase; and you must never allow society to define success for you."

A Very Special "Thank You"

Thank you for purchasing *Resilient As F*ck*.

Visit **www.8figured.com** now to register your book and receive these exclusive bonuses:

You'll get:

- Access to join the *8Figured Body Program* and receive $100 off the total investment.
- 25% off 8Figured brand apparel.
- Free, 2-month subscription to the 8Figured Body private Facebook Health & Wellness Group.

Follow me on Instagram: @iamdeblair
LinkedIn: DeBlair F. Tate

Stay up to date by joining the community. Using your cell phone, text **ResilientAF** to 770-685-6709, and follow the prompts.